FUNDAMENTALS

OF

JEWISH
MYSTICISM
AND
KABBALAH

FUNDAMENTALS
OF
JEWISH
MYSTICISM
AND
KABBALAH

RON H. FELDMAN

THE CROSSING PRESS
FREEDOM, CALIFORNIA

For information on bulk purchases or group discounts for this and other
Crossing Press titles, please contact our Special Sales Manager at
800/777-1048

Visit our Web site on the Internet: www.crossingpress.com

Library of Congress Cataloging-in-Publication Data
Feldman, Ron H.
    Fundamentals of Jewish mysticism and Kabbalah / Ron Feldman.
        p. cm.
    Includes bibliographical references.
    ISBN 1-58091-049-1
    1. Cabala--Outlines, syllabi, etc. 2. Mysticism--Judaism-
-Outlines, syllabi, etc. I. Title.
BM526.F45   1999
296.7'12--DC21   98-52711
                                                CIP

*For my parents, Saul and Claire Feldman, my source;
and my daughter, Kalia, my continuity;
and my wife, Laura Binah, the weaver;
all of us, strands in the braid of the generations.*

Table of Contents

List of Figures and Tables

A Note on Hebrew Usage in this Book

Hebrew is the language of Torah, the Jewish Bible, and the language of the kabbalists who believe that the words and the letters of the Torah are God-given and retain divine potencies. Thus, the writer on Kabbalah is torn between translation, which loses the essential Hebrew aspect of the language; transliteration, which retains the Hebrew sound but no meaning for the English reader; and using the original Hebrew, which can be even more obscure.

While I occasionally include the Hebrew for purposes of illustration, clarification, and a tie to the original sources, I have adopted a hyphenated "*transliteration*-translation" format, with the hope of conveying both the Hebrew sound and the English meaning of the words. While a bit cumbersome, my experience is that it is the best compromise for actual readability of the text, making it unnecessary for the reader to flip back and forth to a glossary.

A Note on Historical Dates

When specifying historical dates, it is common in the west to write "BC" or "AD" which are abbreviations for "Before Christ" and "Anno Domini" (Year of Our Lord). These terms assume a Christian belief that Jews do not share. Therefore, I will use the scholarly terms, BCE (Before Common Era) and CE (Common Era).

Preface—Why Study Kabbalah Today?

For each soul has a unique portion in the Torah.(Rabbi
Moses Cordovero, _Or Ne'erav_)[1]

There was a time when the study of Kabbalah was limited to
Jewish men who were steeped in Jewish learning, well versed
in the Bible, Talmud, their numerous commentaries, and the
rules governing Jewish ritual and religious life. Indeed, there
are some within the Orthodox community today who continue to insist on these preconditions.

However, most Orthodox Jews today—like most Reform,
Conservative non-denominational, or secular Jews—are not
concerned with Kabbalah, a practice which mostly faded
away during the last few hundred years. Elements of Kabbalah
were maintained in the Hasidic communities of Eastern
Europe and the _Mizrahi_-Oriental Jewish communities of
North Africa and the Middle East.* The Eastern European
communities were destroyed in the Holocaust, along with
most of their spiritual masters. Today's descendants of the
Eastern European Hasidic traditions exist mainly in the
United States and Israel, while most of the _Mizrahi_ communities moved to Israel over the last fifty years. Overall,

* _Mizrahi_-Oriental Jews are sometimes mistakenly referred to as Sephardic.
The Sephardim are descended from Spanish Jews, who were expelled from
Spain in 1492. Many Sephardic customs were adopted by _Mizrahi_-Oriental
communities, whose communities from North Africa and the Middle East
often predate the Spanish Expulsion.

however, these constitute but a small percentage of the Jewish community.

The twentieth century has also seen the growth of the academic study of Kabbalah, with a focus on recovering and deciphering the meaning of Jewish mystical texts from the Rabbinic (first century BCE–sixth century CE) to the Middle Ages (seventh–fifteenth centuries) and Early Modern Periods (sixteenth–nineteenth centuries). The goal of this study is to understand the role mysticism has played in the religious, intellectual, and social history of the Jews.

As with any study it is important to place yourself within a context, and within Kabbalah it is important that you, the reader, know the stance from which I, the author, speak. Indeed, I would caution you to discover this about any book you read about Kabbalah, for there are many who claim an exclusivity to their understanding of kabbalistic truths or secrets. Kabbalah is nothing if not a chain of tradition—but, in fact, it is more like a braid than a chain, with many strands composing it, and it is important to locate oneself in that braid. My belief is that so many strands in the braid have been broken that today is a time for grasping those within our reach, adding new thread, and reweaving the braid to make it strong enough for many to hold onto.

For myself, I am largely sympathetic to the Jewish Renewal's approach to Kabbalah, whose leading proponent is Rabbi Zalman Schachter-Shalomi. Other teachers (not all of whom identify with Jewish Renewal) whom I have had the privilege to learn with in person include Phyllis Ocean Berman, Diane Bloomfield, Yitzhak Buxbaum, Rabbi Shlomo Carlebach *(z"l)**, Eli Cohen, Joseph-Mark Cohen, Rabbi David A. Cooper, Rabbi Ted Falcon, Rabbi Steven Fisdel, Rabbi Shefa Gold, Eve Ilsen, Rabbi Lawrence Kushner, Rabbi Miles Krassen, Rabbi Leah Novick, Rabbi Jonathan Omer-Man, Rabbi Marcia Prager, Rabbi Jeff Roth, Rabbi Arthur Ocean Waskow, Rabbi Shohama Wiener, Rabbi Gershon Winkler, Rabbi David Wolfe-Blank *(z"l)*, and Rabbi Dovid Zeller. In particular I want to thank Professor Daniel C. Matt for reading an early draft of a portion of the manuscript and giving numerous suggestions for improvement. I thank them all for the opportunity to learn from their wisdom, while I take full responsibility for the shortcomings herein. Most important of all, I must thank my wife, Laura Binah Feldman, who is my constant partner in exploring the depths of Kabbalah and from whose deep understanding I have learned the most.

For me, the wisdom of the Renewal movement is that it blends elements of the Hasidic tradition, academic scholarship, and modern sensibilities. This especially includes attitudes that incorporate gender equality, an environmental perspective, an openness to dialogue with other spiritual traditions, with an overall goal of sharing and evolving spiritual

---

* *Z"l* is a Hebrew abbreviation for *zichrono l'bracha*, "may his memory be a blessing," and is recited after saying the name of someone who is dead.

practices based on Kabbalah that speak to people in our contemporary modern culture. There is also a respect for the individual and his/her ability to learn and teach, who is not asked to enter a cult that depends on and defers to the wisdom of one Rabbinic master who is considered holy. Just as the destruction of the First Temple ended the age of Prophecy, I believe that the Holocaust ended the era of Rebbes, the charismatic Rabbis who were the leaders of Hasidic sects. As Rabbi Zalman Schachter-Shalomi has said, in this more democratic and egalitarian era we need to learn to be Rebbes to each other, finding the "rebbe spark" within each of us.

It must be remembered that the Holocaust did more than destroy the spiritual centers of Judaism in Europe; it destroyed the interest of most Jews in a spiritual life. On the religious level one couldn't avoid asking the obvious question: If there is a God, how could the Holocaust happen? The answers given by the masses of Jews were, for the most part, either a) God doesn't exist, or, b) if God does exist, He/She/It is not relevant to our life on this earth.

The Jewish people found an answer, and an escape, from this spiritual conundrum by conversion to the cause of Zionism, which provided a clear focus for social and political action. Physical survival became the aim of world Jewry; creating and supporting the State of Israel was the means to that goal, and for many Jews this struggle filled the spiritual vacuum that remained after the Holocaust.

But for Jews today the security of the State of Israel has seemed a growing certainty at the same time that diaspora Jews feel safer in their own lands. The very success of the cause of Israel and the fight against antisemitism and anti-Zionism has produced a new situation where Jews are able to ask a new question: Survival for what? In Israel, America, and other countries this has meant a turn towards spirituality, a dimension of Judaism that had been in the background for over fifty years.

During those fifty years most Jews have become increasingly unreligious in any traditional orthodox sense, an acceleration of a trend that had already been in progress. Most Jews are very distant from even minimal Jewish practice and knowledge, let alone the level of knowledge that was assumed by the classical kabbalists. Yet the spiritual dimension of life explored by the kabbalists is what contemporary Jews, and non-Jews, are searching for in ever greater numbers.

Kabbalah started out as complex esoteric practices of a small elite of educated men. When the medieval kabbalists wrote, the Jewish community was physically much smaller, and all Jews were subject to Jewish law. There was a relative homogeneity in Jewish practice that is no longer the case today. Later, the Hasidic movement of the eighteenth and nineteenth centuries simplified and popularized kabbalistic concepts as central tools for spiritual revival. Hasidism's radical spiritual and psychological emphasis was strongly opposed by many rabbis of that time. Of course, by the standards of today's culture the surviving communities of traditional Hasidim are the conservatives.

The challenge now is how to enter into a dialogue with the kabbalists and their teachings, when their language and world-view was so different from our own. While some Jews become *Baalei Teshuvah*-masters of return—that is, converts to Jewish Orthodoxy—most, including myself, do not find this a satisfying spiritual path. Most of us prefer to leap forward rather than turn back. Nor can the strictly academic path, with its emphasis on intellect over experience, provide answers to spiritual questions.

A lost tradition that is too esoteric or foreign cannot answer people's needs. Yet one must recognize the danger that oversimplification may betray the tradition in the mistaken hope of connecting people to it. This struggle between the past and the future has been ongoing throughout Jewish history, with the only constant being the conversation itself.

Every person who transmits a tradition is a mediator, taking their understanding of what they have received and combining it with their own insights and experience. My goal in this small volume is to bring some of what was and what is to the reader's awareness, with faith that this will facilitate our discovery together of what might yet be. I hope that this book will open a door for you into the hidden courtyard of the Kabbalah, and that those of you who enter will find places to sit, other books to study, and a community with whom you can practice and learn.

Introduction: What Is the Kabbalah?

Imitate your creator. Then you will enter the mystery of the supernal form, the divine image in which you were created.
(Rabbi Moses Cordovero, The Palm Tree of Devorah)[2]

The Hebrew word *Kabbalah* means "that which is received" and refers to a broad range of Jewish mystical traditions and texts which have come down to us over the centuries. But *Kabbalah* also means "receiving," and the kabbalist—one who practices the Kabbalah—believes the possibility of receiving cosmic truths is available at every moment, if we are only properly attuned and receptive.

On the psychospiritual level the Kabbalah—including its literature and spiritual practices, like prayer, meditation, chanting, breath control, and fasting—can best be understood as Jewish teachings and tools for attaining transcendence, or "God-consciousness."[3] The Kabbalah's promise and premise is that, by following these practices, the devotee will not only receive and understand the ancient laws and wisdom as written, but receive a personal experience of *devekut*-adherence (closeness to God), a peak experience that allows the seeker to glimpse the oneness of all creation and experience eternity. "In the beginning God created the heaven and the earth" (Genesis 1:1). This process of creation described in the first line of the Bible never stopped; it is ongoing—it is *now*!

While our mundane daily life is in the world of distinctions and separation, the kabbalist knows that, when seen properly, these distinctions disappear. Kabbalists believe that commitment to these practices is not only a way of overcoming the personal isolation we feel in this world of duality, but also a way of healing, repairing, and rebalancing the universe as a whole, a process known as *tikkun olam*—repair of the world.

On one level Kabbalah can be seen as a kind of Jewish psychology, where the kabbalist's ultimate goal is personal spiritual growth, seen as loss of the ego so that one can experience closeness to God. Kabbalists are not satisfied with remembering and interpreting the reports of spiritual encounters by biblical figures; they want to have those ecstatic experiences themselves. Of course, anyone who establishes their own channel to God may be tempted to reject the cultural and legal traditions upon which society is based, and Kabbalah was sometimes considered dangerous by legalists and rationalists within the Jewish world. This was probably the source of the well-known rule that Kabbalah should only be studied by a married man over forty years old, although in fact many kabbalists were much younger. Kabbalists made strong efforts to defend their practices by referring to sacred textual sources. Kabbalah is a radical way of thinking cloaked in traditional terminology; revolutionary concepts claiming ancient tradition and lineage.

Over the centuries kabbalists, like other Jewish scholars, were almost always men. Indeed, the great modern scholar of Kabbalah, Gershom Scholem, writes that, "both historically and metaphysically it is a masculine doctrine, made for men and by men. The long history of Jewish mysticism shows no trace of feminine influence."[4] By this he means that it is a strongly androcentric, patriarchal tradition in which women played almost no role. Unlike well known female Christian mystics, such as Teresa of Avila or Hildegaard of Bingen, there may have been women kabbalists, but we can safely (and unfortunately) say that there is no known documentation by women or reflecting a woman's perspective prior to the eighteenth century, and very little prior to our own generation. Like much else about women's life and perspective, there was possibly a tradition that has been lost or hidden, which remains to be recovered.[5]

Today, however, women are taking an active role in the revival of Kabbalah. To counterbalance the androcentric views of traditional kabbalists, many modern kabbalists have re-emphasized and expanded the traditional kabbalistic concept of the *Shekhinah*-Presence, the feminine presence of God in our universe. Gender was important in traditional Kabbalah, which tended to see the feminine as physical, while masculine was associated with the spirit. Some of today's kabbalists believe this feminine position is a virtue, believing that spiritual life can be attained via the celebration of the physical rather than by its negation, and find a basis for this in some of the writings and practices of the kabbalists. Motivated both by feminism and environmentalism, Rabbi Zalman Schachter-Shalomi has written that Kabbalah is evolving as "we are entering the phase of the divinization of the planet."[6]

There are many dimensions to Kabbalah, and many ways to enter into the world of kabbalistic concepts. As for many other religious traditions, it is important to distinguish between two aspects: the inner experience and the outer form. On the one hand there is the inner personal experience of the transcendent. This experiential trend within Kabbalah, which scholars tend to refer to as *ecstatic*, assumes that such an experience is available and aims at accessing this realm. The focus here is on practices that can lead the kabbalist on a path to personal revelation and closeness to God. There are some writings and teachings in this area that instruct the student on the path, but inevitably these experiences are intrinsically personal and communicable only by image and metaphor. Many of these teachings were traditionally passed on orally from master to student and rarely committed to paper, due both to their intrinsically experiential nature and to the possibility of misinterpretation.

On the other hand, there is the outer tradition of Kabbalah that includes the evolution of rituals, traditions, and texts—indeed, a whole culture—which have evolved and accrued over hundreds of years. This material is often referred to by scholars as *theosophical* (the theory of the elaborate structure of the divine world) and *theurgical* (rituals aimed at affecting God and perfecting a state of cosmic harmony). This theoretical side of Kabbalah developed many esoteric doctrines regarding the hidden life of God and the relation of God to humanity and creation, including cosmology, angelology, and magic. Due to this philosophical aspect, much of the older written material on Kabbalah is of this type. Indeed, the emphasis of much of this writing was on mystical explanations and interpretations of *halakhah*, the laws of Jewish conduct that the Rabbinic authorities derived from the Torah and Talmud. These laws include, for example, the dietary laws of keeping kosher, the restriction of work on the *shabbat*-sabbath, the eating of matzoh on *Pesach*-Passover, and various other ritual and holiday regulations.[7]

These two strains evolved simultaneously, sometimes in discord and sometimes in harmony. Sometimes the distinction was self-conscious, but often the two aspects are combined in a confusing fashion.[8] Some of the more theosophical texts were no doubt the result of ecstatic experience, and were subsequently used as guides by others to attaining such experiences. Ezekiel's biblical description of the Throne or Chariot of God is one such example. Because of the perceived dangers of misuse—both to the individual who might get hurt if not properly guided, or to the world if the information was used for evil ends—manuscripts were often written in a code only understandable to the initiated, and many ideas and practices were secrets passed from master to student. Indeed, one of the more cryptic phrases used in kabbalistic literature is, "the one who understands will understand." Much was certainly lost over the generations, but much was also preserved due to the Jewish tradition of commentary. Thus, various kabbalistic books such as the _Zohar_-Brightness and _Sefer Yetzirah_-Book of Formation were in turn the subject of numerous Rabbinical commentaries and interpretations.

One difficulty for many people who approach Kabbalah today is the terminology used in the older literature, and, traditionally, the older a text is, the more important and venerated it is. Our egalitarian and feminist cultural sensibility renders many ancient and medieval images of God such as "King" and "Lord" quite alienating, and these terms are used regularly in the pre-modern texts.

While the kabbalists used these terms to emphasize the awesome nature of God, they did not think of God exclusively as some Being or Force that is separate from and above us. Indeed, part of the radical nature of Kabbalah is the immanent notion that God is everywhere and in everything. The God of the kabbalists is not only the Creator, but also a personal, inward experience of Being. Creation is not over; it unfolds at every moment. For the kabbalist, God is not only the philosopher's First Cause, but also a continuing process. For the kabbalist, God is not a noun, but a verb.[9] According to Genesis, humans were created in God's image; thus, the unfolding of God's manifestation in creation is imitated by us in a parallel unfolding of our own selves.

Jewish Mystical Texts and Practices

Mysticism in the Bible

> Moses said, "I must turn aside to look at this marvelous sight; why doesn't the bush burn up?" When the Lord saw that he had turned aside to look, God called to him out of the bush: "Moses! Moses!" He answered, "Here I am." And He said, "Do not come closer. Remove your sandals from your feet, for the place on which you stand is holy ground." (Exodus 3:3–5)

The Bible, of course, is the core text for all Kabbalah, and it is full of reports of magical, miraculous, and mystical occurrences. There are numerous accounts of God speaking to individuals, either directly (e.g., Abraham, Moses), through dreams (e.g., Jacob, Joseph) or via an angelic representative (e.g., Abraham and Sara, Jacob). There is the revelation of the Ten Commandments at Mount Sinai, which was perceived by everyone present. There are also stories of divination through the casting of lots in the stories of Esther and Jonah, and the *urim* and *thumim*, divination devices kept in a bag behind the *ephod*-vest of the High Priest. As Jacob and Moses discovered in the most desolate of places, the fundamental realization is that the sacred dimension is available to us at any place and time, if only we are prepared to receive it.

The Torah is read in the synagogue on a yearly cycle that begins and ends on the autumn holiday of *Simhat Torah*-Joy in the Torah. For each week of the year there is a *parsha*-portion that is read (because the number of weeks of the year can vary in the Jewish calendar, there are complicated rules for dividing up the readings in years of various lengths). Kabbalists use the Torah in a way similar to how astrological birthcharts and weekly horoscopes are used. It is thought that the *parsha*-portion of the Torah read on the *shabbat*-sabbath of your birth—that is, the *shabbat*-sabbath that follows your birthday—contains special information concerning your soul and the path of your life. The *parsha*-portion of each week is said to contain information to help you through the crises and opportunities that life presents.

Ma'aseh Merkavah—The Workings of the Chariot

> When I was in the community of exiles by the Chebar river, the heavens opened and I saw visions of God. (Ezekiel 1:1)

> I looked, and lo, a stormy wind came sweeping out of the north, a huge cloud and flashing fire, surrounded by a radiance; and in the center of it, in the center of the fire, a gleam as of amber. In the center of it were also the figures of four creatures. (Ezekiel 1:4–5)

> Above the expanse over their heads was the semblance of a throne, in appearance like sapphire; and on top, upon this semblance of a throne, there was the semblance of a human form....When I beheld it, I flung myself down on my face. And I heard the voice of someone speaking. (Ezekiel 1:26–28)

For Jewish mystics, one of the most important stories is the revelation of Ezekiel, who perceived the heavenly chariot, also known as the Throne of God. This became the core for the school known as the *ma'aseh merkavah*-Workings of the Chariot. Ezekiel's description came to be seen as the model of the prophetic experience, revealed just before the destruction of the First Temple, which ended the age of Prophecy. For over one thousand years, from the first century BCE until the tenth century CE, the *ma'aseh merkavah*-Workings of the Chariot was the primary path of the Jewish mystics.

A mystical school grew up around Ezekiel's vision, and its practitioners aimed at retracing his steps, his map of how to get close to God. There is a very large literature that comments and expands upon Ezekiel's vision. Early on it was expanded by attributing to Ezekiel a vision of the seven heavens or heavenly halls. One passage, for example, attributes the following:

> Thus Ezekiel stood beside the river Chebar gazing into the water and the seven heavens were opened to him so that he saw the Glory of the Holy One, blessed be He, the *hayyot,* the ministering angels, the angelic hosts, the seraphim, those of sparkling wings, all attached to the *merkavah.* They passed by in heaven while Ezekiel saw them (reflected) in the water.[10]

The *ma'aseh merkavah*-Workings of the Chariot mystics developed breathing, postures, and chanting practices to assist them in their visionary quest. Hai Gaon, who lived in the ninth century CE, gave this description of practices of this school:

> You may perhaps know that many of the Sages hold that when a man is worthy and blessed with certain qualities and he wishes to gaze at the heavenly chariot and the halls of the angels on high, he must follow certain exercises. He must fast for a specified number of days, he must place his head between his knees whispering softly to himself the while certain praises of God with his face towards the ground. As a result he will gaze in the innermost recesses of his heart and it will seem as if he saw the seven halls with his own eyes, moving from hall to hall to observe that which is therein to be found.[11]

These "chariot gazers" were known as the *yordei ha-merkavah,* "those who descend to the chariot." The chariot was not something they traveled in, but was God's heavenly throne that the mystic aimed to approach, thereby obtaining a view of God's majesty and the secrets of the heavenly realm. This was a path to personal enlightenment, granted in full only to the most saintly and deserving.

One of the best known instances of this school is the Talmudic story that dates from the second century CE about four rabbis who entered the *Pardes*, originally a Persian word—which means orchard or garden, and from which the word paradise derives. In this case the reference is to God's Garden, a mystical paradise. There are various interpretations of this piece, but academic scholars believe that this was a reflection of the practices of *merkavah* school, and that the four rabbis were gazing at God's chariot.

> Our Rabbis taught: Four entered an orchard and these are they: Ben Azzai, Ben Zoma, Aher, and Rabbi Akiva. Rabbi Akiva said to them: "When you reach the stones of pure marble, do not say: 'Water, water!' For it is said 'He that speaks falsehood shall not be established before my eyes.'" Ben Azzai gazed and died. Of him Scripture says: "Precious in the sight of the Lord is the death of his saints." Ben Zoma gazed and was stricken. Of him Scripture says: "Have you found honey? Eat as much as is sufficient for you, lest you be filled therewith, and vomit it." Aher cut down the shoots. Rabbi Akiva departed in peace. (*Hagigah* 14b)[12]

The passage is a bit opaque due to its use of metaphor. The traditional interpretation is that it was time for Ben Azzai to die, but God first granted him a vision of the *merkavah*. Ben

Zoma, on the other hand, beheld the splendor but was overwhelmed and went mad. Aher, which means "the other" became a dualist, believing in two divine powers as the source of good and evil, a Zoroastrian concept that had echoes throughout the ancient world, including the Dead Sea sect; cutting the shoots is a metaphor for his apostasy from Jewish monotheism.

Thus, the passage is a warning to those who would dabble in mysticism without proper training and guidance, for only one of the four, Rabbi Akiva, came out in peace, which in Hebrew is *shalom*, meaning peace in the sense of wholeness and completion. Yet it is also a reflection of the fact that the Talmud takes mystical practices very seriously, which is why there is such a stern warning to do it right.

Ma'aseh Bereshit—The Workings of Creation

> With thirty-two mystical paths of wisdom engraved Yah...
> And He created His universe with three *seferim*-books,
> with *sefer*-book,
> with *sefar*-counting
> and with *sippur*-telling. (*Sefer Yetzirah* 1:1)
>
> Ten *sefirot*-emanations of Nothingness
> And *twenty*-two Foundation Letters (*Sefer Yetzirah* 1:2)[13]

The other ancient branch of Jewish mysticism is *ma'aseh bereshit*-Workings of Creation. Its core document is the *Sefer Yetzirah*-Book of Formation, one of the oldest kabbalistic texts. Kabbalists have traditionally attributed the book to Abraham while academic scholars believe it was first written down in Palestine some time between the third and sixth century CE. The _Sefer Yetzirah_-Book of Formation is the source for a number of critical kabbalistic concepts which evolved and accumulated over the centuries as numerous commentaries were written, amplifying its brief and cryptic verses.

While _Genesis_ merely reports that creation occurred by God's speech, the _Sefer Yetzirah_-Book of Formation asserts that there were thirty-two tools of creation, the ten numbers and the twenty-two letters of the Hebrew alphabet, and that God's "speech" was actually a communication, a "telling," that was manifested by the combination and permutation of these primordial numbers and letters. This resulted in the dimensions of space, time, and spirit as well as the three aspects of the letters themselves: their form, numerical value, and pronunciation. This divine speech determined the structure of the universe including time, the seven days of the week, the six directions, the four elements, the seasons of the year, the astrological months and houses, and the organs of the body.

The Hebrew Alphabet

בראשית ברא אלהים את השמים ואת הארץ

Bereshit bara Elohim et ha-shamayim v'et ha-aretz.

In the beginning God created the heaven and the earth. (Genesis 1:1)

For kabbalists, the Hebrew letters are the tools of creation that God used to speak the universe into existence (see Table 1: The Hebrew Alphabet). This is expressed in the first verse of the Torah, shown above. The _Zohar_-Brightness explains their importance by commenting on the first verse of the Torah:

> Et—when He took all these letters, [et] comprised all the letters, beginning and end. (_Zohar_ 1: 15b)[14]

Et-את is an interesting linguistic structure that points to the prefix hey-ה, which is the "the" of the following noun. However, et-את is itself untranslatable. Et-את is a grammatical form emphasizing definitiveness. What is important for the kabbalist is that et-את symbolizes the Hebrew alphabet as a whole because it is spelled by א-alef and ת-tav, the first and last letters of the alphabet. The _Zohar_-Brightness understands this passage as, "In the beginning God created et." That is, before God could even speak the world into being the letters had to be created so speech would be possible; creation was only possible when the infinity of God's being had congealed into a degree of definiteness and distinction, which was the alphabet. For the kabbalist, the Hebrew letters are the tools of creation.

Kabbalists believe that the letters represent actual forces and energies; they exist on a metaphysical plane, and

Letter	Name	Literal Meaning	Sound	Numerical Value
א	Alef	Ox	silent	1
ב	Bet	House	B,V	2
ג	Gimmel	Camel	G, GH	3
ד	Dalet	Door	D,Dh	4
ה	Hey	Window	H	5
ו	Vav	Hook	V (W)	6
ז	Zayin	Weapon	Z	7
ח	Het	Fence	Kh	8
ט	Tet	Snake	T	9
י	Yod	Hand	Y (I)	10
כ	Kaf	Palm of Hand	K, Kh	20
ל	Lamed	Ox-goad	L	30
מ	Mem	Water	M	40
נ	Nun	Fish	N	50
ס	Samekh	Support	S	60
ע	Ayin	Eye	silent	70
פ	Peh	Mouth	P,Ph	80
צ	Tsadi	Fish-hook	Tz	90
ק	Kuf	Back of head	K (Q)	100
ר	Resh	Head	R,Rh	200
ש	Shin	Tooth	Sh (S)	300
ת	Tav	Cross	T,Th	400

existed there before their physical manifestation, just as any idea exists in the mind before it can be manifested in the physical realm. For kabbalists, the Hebrew letters themselves are considered holy, and many kabbalistic meditations focus on Hebrew letters, their shapes and meanings. Exploring the depths of the alphabet itself is therefore a favorite kabbalistic quest.

Thus, while on the surface *Sefer Yetzirah*-Book of Formation seems to be primarily a theosophical document, expanding on the first verse of the Torah by detailing how God created the universe and the meaning behind some of the structures we experience, it also came to be understood as a guide to meditation. Genesis (1:27) reports that "God created the human in His image." The kabbalistic view is that humans can become closer to God by emulating God's methods of manifesting the energies of creation. In particular, Abraham Abulafia derived his methods of mediation based on letter permutations, chanting, and head motions from the *Sefer Yetzirah*-Book of Formation.[15] The Talmud reports that similar methods were used in a magical way for creating a *golem*, an animated clay figure, but this was a rare ability only available to a few deserving initiates.[16]

The *Sefirot*-Emanations

It is in the *Sefer Yetzirah*-Book of Formation that the term *sefirot*-emanations is first used in Hebrew literature. *Sefirot* (plural of *sefirah*) is one of those wonderful words that has multiple layers of meaning. On a simple level it means number or cipher, but with an implication of sequence and counting. This implies an affinity for the Pythagorean notion that numbers themselves possess metaphysical dimensions. Later Kabbalists also connected *sefirah*-emanation to *sapir*-sapphire, which the Torah reports as the color of Mt. Sinai (Exodus 24:10) and the Throne of God (Ezekiel 1:26) during those mystical encounters. The *sapir*-sapphire of antiquity was the gem we today call *lapis lazuli,* a deep blue stone with gold and white flecks that make it look like the heavens.[17] The *Sefer Bahir*-Book of Clarity further identifies this color with the sea, the sky, and the four blue threads of the *tzitzit*-fringes placed on the corners of the prayer shawl (Num. 15:38).[18]

While the *sefirot*-emanations in the <u>Sefer Yetzirah</u>-Book of Formation initially referred to the first ten numbers or digits, the concept evolved by the time of the <u>Zohar</u>-Brightness into representing stages of God's biography, of what God did "behind the scenes" in order to create the universe. Kabbalists are aware of the danger that the *sefirot*-emanations might be mistaken for independent entities and that there is a danger of idolatrous worship of the *sefirot*-emanations rather than God. As emanations of God they are clearly not God although they are close to God, or manifestations of aspects of God. The fact that the *sefirot*-emanations and letters imply sequence and structure means that they exist within time, and thus are not identical to God, who created time. This is the way kabbalists reconcile a potentially pantheistic system to monotheism.

The transcendent God remains the ultimate source of these *sefirot*-emanations and is called the *Ein Sof*-Infinite (literally "without end"). Virtually nothing can be said about the *Ein Sof*-Infinite because it is so far beyond human intelligibility. We cannot apprehend the *Ein Sof*-Infinite, only the lower manifestations through which it creates and acts vis-a-vis the universe. This infinite aspect of God, which cannot be contained, is also known as *Ayin*-Nothingness; this is the mysterious point before the first point of light, the *Ayin*-Nothingness pregnant with the potential of the *Ein Sof*-Infinite.

The *sefirot*-emanations emerge from the *Ein Sof*-Infinite as tools of creation. They draw all their energy from the *Ein Sof*-Infinite, and have no independent existence. To use a modern metaphor, the *sefirot*-emanations can be viewed as a series of step-down transformers, reducing the infinite energy of the *Ein Sof*-Infinite to tools useful for creating the universe of distinctions and difference. The *sefirot*-emanations represent stages in the process of Creation, and their order represents the evolutionary sequence of Becoming. Since Creation is happening continuously, the *sefirot*-emanations describe both Being and Becoming as one unified process that continues to happen at every moment.

The Hebrew names of the *sefirot*-emanations are derived from various biblical passages, and meanings of the names themselves are not always that clear; indeed, some *sefirot*-emanations have multiple names, each shedding a different light on its function. Each *sefirah*-emanations is associated with a particular biblical name of God, and it is thought that when the Torah records a particular name this indicates that God is acting with the energy of its *sefirah*-emanations. Thus, much kabbalistic Torah commentary is focused on explaining the *sefirot*-emanations and their relationship to each other. Many apparently insignificant Torah passages are interpreted to reveal deep meaning concerning the interaction of the *sefirot*-emanations.

The Kabbalistic "Tree-of-Life"

The ten *sefirot*-emanations have been depicted in numerous patterns in kabbalistic literature. They are commonly seen as concentric circles, or as aspects of the *menorah*-candelabra used in the Temple, probably Judaism's most ancient symbol. The most popular and best known pattern of the *sefirot*-emanations is the kabbalistic "Tree-of-Life." This represents the "thirty-two mystical paths"—the ten *sefirot*-emanations and twenty-two letters—and their interrelationship. Figure 1: The Kabbalistic "Tree-of-Life" shows the thirty-two paths according to Rabbi Isaac Luria. The ten *sefirot*-emanations, represented by circles (it should be noted that there is no

FIGURE 1: THE KABBALISTIC TREE-OF-LIFE

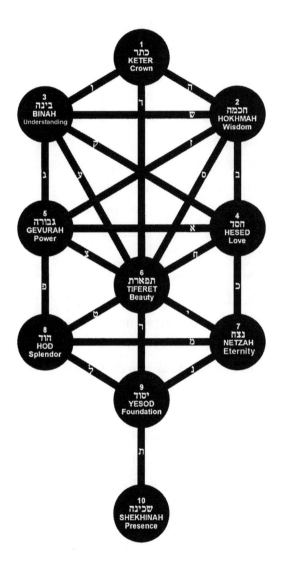

linguistic connection between the Hebrew *sefirah*-emanations and the English "sphere"), are connected by twenty-two lines, each associated with a Hebrew letter. Together, these thirty-two paths can be thought of as states of consciousness, as energetic flows, and as archetypal divine qualities. The *Sefer Yetzirah*-Book of Formation makes a distinction between the *sefirot*-emanations and letters: While the letters are a concept that do have physical form, the *sefirot*-emanations are described as "*sefirot* of nothingness," meaning that they are concepts without any physical substance or form. While the letters are expressible, the *sefirot*-emanations are ultimately beyond our comprehension, with names but without sound or form.

The *Sefer Bahir*-Book of Clarity is the earliest kabbalistic text that describes these *sefirot*-emanations as a "Tree-of-Life," alluding to the Garden of Eden story in Genesis, where Adam and Eve ate the fruit from the "Tree-of-Knowledge" but were expelled before they were able to eat from the "Tree-of-Life." The thirty-two threads of the *tzitzit*-fringes are also associated with the thirty-two mystical paths. The Torah itself is also equated with the Tree-of-Life (Proverbs 3:18).

The Tree-of-Life is also known as the *Adam Kadmon*-Primordial Human, for the human body, created in the image of God, is thought to be an echo of this original image comprised of the *sefirot*-emanations. Thus, the first *sefirah*-emanation is usually known as *Keter*-Crown because it is the top of the head of the primordial Adam, whose crown receives the divine influx of energy from the *Ein Sof*-Infinite. *Hokhmah*-Wisdom, the second *sefirah*-emanation, emerges from *Keter*-Crown as a point of light. This radiates a circle, which becomes the third *sefirah*-emanation, *Binah*-Understanding. *Hokhmah*-Wisdom is also the Divine Father, who fertilizes *Binah*-Understanding, the Divine Mother, in whose womb the seven lower *sefirot*-emanations are conceived and to whom she gives birth. This first triad is thought of as the head of *Adam Kadmon*-Primordial Human.

Hesed-Love, *Gevurah*-Power, and *Tiferet*-Beauty are the next triad to be born. The free-flowing energy of *Hesed*-Love must be contained by the restraint and severity of *Gevurah*-Power (also known as *Din*-Judgment), in order for creation to function, and are seen as the right and left arm of *Adam Kadmon*-Primordial Human. Evil is thought to arise when an overabundance of *Gevurah*-Power overwhelms *Hesed*-Love. Ideally a balance is achieved so that energy flows through to *Tiferet*-Beauty, the central *sefirah*-emanation and the heart of *Adam Kadmon*-Primordial Human, which is identified with the sun and *YHVH*-The Name.

The seventh, eighth, and ninth *sefirot*-emanations make up the third triad of *Netzakh*-Eternity, *Hod*-Splendor and *Yesod*-Foundation. *Netzakh*-Eternity and *Hod*-Splendor make up the right and left legs of *Adam Kadmon*-Primordial Human while *Yesod*-Foundation is the cosmic phallus. All of the cosmic energy of the preceding *sefirot*-emanations are channeled through *Yesod*-Foundation to the tenth *sefirah*-emanation, *Shekhinah*-Presence, also known as *Malkhut*-Kingdom. *Shekhinah*-Presence is the daughter of *Binah*-Understanding and the bride of *Tiferet*-Beauty, which is identified with the *YHVH*-The Name. Through righteous acts, humans can stimulate *Yesod*-Foundation, also known as *Tsadik*-Righteous One, bringing about the cosmic coupling of *Tiferet*-Beauty and *Shekhinah*-Presence. This increases the flow of positive energy into our physical world, which is the realm in which *Shekhinah*-Presence reigns as Queen. This is why *Shekhinah*-Presence is variously identified in the body of *Adam Kadmon*-Primordial Human with the cosmic yoni that receives the influx from *YHVH*-The Name, or with the feet that contact the earth.

Although the image of the Tree-of-Life seems hierarchical, the flow is actually going both ways along all the paths all the time. While the energy from God to creation is channeled down through the paths, every element of creation has a spark of the divine, and the purpose of this spark is to return to its Creator and Source.

The Tree-of-Life is also sometimes seen as "Jacob's ladder," and one way for the individual kabbalist to raise the holy sparks of his/her soul to achieve a mystical experience of *devekut*-adherence to God is to ascend towards God via the ladder of the *sefirot*-emanations through various meditative techniques. One traditional kabbalistic practice, for example, is to focus your study and/or meditation on one or a sequence of the *sefirot*-emanations and/or letters.

"Up" and "down" are not exactly the right terms, for when this two-dimensional image is correctly oriented in our world, it lies flat with the "top" pointing to the east. It is best to think of the Tree-of-Life as a map; although we often speak of "up" or "down" when referring to north and south, this refers to the map, not the terrain. In fact, it is best to think of the Tree-of-Life multidimensionally. The two-dimensional image is just a slice of an n-dimensional vibrating, spinning, spiraling, energy system. It is the primordial pattern that describes the energetic reverberations of the world. In contemporary terms, we can think of the Tree-of-Life as the kabbalist's picture of God's DNA, and therefore the DNA of the universe. The *sefirot*-emanations and letters are like the nucleotides in DNA, the building blocks, the basic patterns which repeat themselves in virtually endless ways to manifest the world in all its variety. It is through the qualities represented by the Tree-of-Life that God creates the universe as we know it—not only historically, but repeatedly, at every moment of existence.

Over the centuries there have been many commentaries expanding on our understanding of the meaning embodied in the symbolism of the *sefirot*-emanations. With so many commentaries over such a long period, it is no surprise that

SEFIRAH HEBREW NAME	כתר	חכמה	בינה	חסד
SEFIRAH NAME TRANSLITERATED	Keter	Hokhmah	Binah	Hesed
SEFIRAH NAME TRANSLATION	Crown (Thought, Enlightenment)	Wisdom, Concept	Understanding, Insight, Comprehension	Love, Loving Kindness, Mercy
NUMBER	1	2	3	4
DAY OF WEEK[19]				Sunday
DAY–CHARACTER[20]	Big Bang: In the Beginning	Tohu, Primal Chaotic Energy	Bohu, Primal Void	Light
COLOR[21]	White	White	White	Purple
BIBLICAL MALE ARCHETYPE[22]				Abraham
BIBLICAL FEMALE ARCHITYPE[23]				Miriam
BODY PART[24]	Top of Head; Skull, Cranium	Right Brain	Left Brain	Right Shoulder, Arm, Lung
DIVINE NAME (HEBREW)[25]	אהיה אשר אהיה	יה	יהוה (אלהים)	אל
DIVINE NAME (TRANSLITERATED)[26]	Ehyeh Asher Ehyeh	Yah	YHVH (read Elohim)	El
JEWISH HOLIDAY[27]	Yom Kippur	Rosh Hashana (First Day)	Rosh Hashanah (Second Day)	Passover
PLANET[28]				Moon (Levana)
ALTERNATE NAMES	Ayin (Nothingness)			Gedulah (Greatness)
DIRECTION[29]	Beginning/Cause	Past	Future	South
ORIENTATION[30]				Right
CONCEPTUAL REPRESENTATION[31]	Will, Purpose	Mind, Axioms	Logic	Giving
GENESIS 1[32]	When God began to create Heaven and earth—the earth being unformed and void, with darkness over the surface of the deep (1:1)	God said, "Let there be light"; and there was light. (1:3)	God said, "Let there be an expanse in the midst of the water, that it may separate water from water." (1:6)	God said, "Let the water below the sky be gathered into one area, that the dry land may appear." (1:9)

גבורה	תפארת	נצח	הוד	יסוד	שכינה
Gevurah	Tiferet	Netzakh	Hod	Yesod	Shekhinah
Power, Strength, Severity, Restraint	Beauty	Eternity, Endurance, Victory	Splendor, Glory	Foundation, Bonding	Presence
5	6	7	8	9	10
Monday	Tuesday	Wednesday	Thursday	Friday	Shabbat
Separation of Waters, Above & Below	Dry Land, Plant Life	Sun, Moon, Stars	Egg-laying Creaters—Birds, Fish, Reptile	Mammals & Humans	Rest, Not-doing
Blue	Green	Yellow	Orange	Red	Brown
Isaac	Jacob	Moses	Aaron	Joseph	David
Leah	Hannah	Rebecca	Sara	Tamar	Rachel
Left Shoulder, Arm, Lung	Heart; Body/Torso	Right Pelvis (Kidney, Thigh, Ovary, Testicle)	Left Pelvis (Kidney, Thigh, Ovary, Testicle)	Genitals; Male Genitals (Also Tongue)	Base of Spine; Female Genitals (Also Mouth, Mate)
אלהים	יהוה (אדני)	אדני צבאות	אלהים צבאות	שדי, אל חי	אדני
Elohim	YHVH (read Adonoy)	Adonoy Tzevaot	Elohim Tzevaot	Shadai or El Hai	Adonoy
Shavuaot	Sukkot	Hanukkah	Purim	Rosh Hodesh	Shabbat
Mars (Maddim)	Sun (Shemesh)	Venus (Noga)	Mercury (Kokhba)	Saturn (Shabtai)	Jupiter (Zedek)
Din (Justice, Judgement), Pakhad (Fear)	Rahamim (Compassion, Charity)			Tsadik (Righteous One)	Malkhut (Kingdom, Kingship, Royalty)
North	East	Up	Down	West	End/Effect
Left	Front	Up	Down	Back	Center, "Palace of the Holy"
Justice, Strength	Harmony, Truth	Victory, Endurance	Submission, Majesty	Covenant, Channel, Axis Mundi, Zion	Receiving, Reciprocity, Jerusalem
And God said, "Let the earth sprout vegetation: seed-bearing plants, fruit trees of every kind on earth that bear fruit with the seed in it." (1:11)	God said: "Let there be lights in the expanse of the sky to separate day from night; they shall serve as signs for the set times—the days and the years; and they shall serve as lights in the expanse of the sky to shine upon the earth." (1:14–15)	God said, "Let the waters bring forth swarms of living creatures, and birds that fly above the earth across the expanse of the sky." (1:20)	God said, "Let the earth bring forth every kind of living creature: cattle, creeping things, and wild beasts of every kind." (1:24)	And God said, "Let us make man in our image, after our likeness. They shall rule the fish of the sea, the birds of the sky, the cattle, the whole earth, and all the creeping things that creep on earth." (1:26)	God said to them, "Be fertile and increase, fill the earth and master it; and rule the fish of the sea, the birds of the sky, and all the living things that creep on earth." (1:28)

there are sometimes conflicting opinions—itself a part of the tradition of Jewish commentary going back to the Talmud. Table 2 organizes some of those associations, giving some idea of the depth of the kabbalistic universe. This may seem complex, but as with any other rich food, eating from the fruit of the Tree-of-Life should only be done in moderation, in the amount that one can digest at any one time.

Historical Development of the Kabbalah

From the Bible to Hasidism

> *YHVH*-The Name appeared to him [Abraham] by the tere-
> binths of Mamre, as he sat at the tent door in the heat of
> the day. (Genesis 18:1)

As an element of Judaism, Kabbalah is no doubt the oldest
continuous mystical tradition in the western world. Direct
encounters with God are reported throughout the Bible.
Indeed, a major focus of the Bible is its record of mystical
experiences from Abraham through the Prophets.
Subsequent mystical literature focuses on esoteric knowledge concerning realms not covered directly in the Bible,
such as speculation concerning God's being, cosmology,
angelology, and magic. These relatively intellectual concerns

exist alongside the more personal mystical practices aimed at individual apprehension of God-consciousness through prayer, contemplation, introspection, illumination, and meditation. The kabbalists traditionally claim that these mystical traditions began with Moses, some claim Abraham, and have been orally passed down over the centuries. Whether this antiquity is historic or legendary, the persistence of the Kabbalah through the centuries attests to its success in stimulating and accessing a real dimension of human experience.

Nevertheless, one must be a bit careful when using the term "Kabbalah." While a mystical tradition has always existed within Judaism, scholars have established that it is only since the thirteenth or fourteenth century that the term "Kabbalah" came to be synonymous with these. Many other terms were also used to designate the mystics, such as "masters of the mystery" or "those who descend to the chariot."[33]

The Kabbalah really gained momentum as a movement during the twelfth and thirteenth centuries CE in southern France and Spain, at the time home to large Jewish communities. Among the many kabbalists of this period was Abraham Abulafia, born in 1240, who is known for his development of meditative, breathing, and visualization techniques focusing on the shapes and energies of the Hebrew letters and the permutations of God's most holy name. The practice of chanting divine names, common in many mystical traditions, is traced back to Abraham by some kabbalists. The aim of these practices was the state of ecstasy attained by the biblical Prophets, a unification with God.[34] Abulafia came to think of himself as a prophet, possibly the messiah, and at one point even tried to convert the Pope![35] He traveled widely, gathering followers but also opponents among the Rabbis of his day.

Around 1280 Moses de Leon, a contemporary of Abulafia, began circulating the first transcriptions of the _Zohar_-Brightness, which eventually became the canon and reference for all subsequent Kabbalah. Although it was attributed to Rabbi Shimon Bar Yohai, a famous rabbi of the second century CE, academicians now believe that the _Zohar_-Brightness was composed (or, if written today, we might call it "channeled") by Moses de Leon. Another major Spanish kabbalist was Joseph Gikatilla, a student of Abulafia and a friend of Moses de Leon. His most famous work is _Sha'are Orah_-Gates of Light, in which he combines the use of holy names with a model of the _sefirot_-emanations, all wrapped up in thick references to the Torah and other kabbalistic works.

The influence of the Kabbalah increased following the Spanish expulsion of the Jews in 1492, when Spanish Jewry was dispersed throughout Europe and the Mediterranean basin. The impact of the expulsion and the accompanying persecution by the Inquisition of Jews who had converted to

Catholicism under duress was comparable to the trauma of the Holocaust in our own generation.

One place that welcomed the Jews of that time was the Ottoman Empire, which controlled most of the eastern Mediterranean, including the Land of Israel. In the Galilean town of Safed, near the purported tomb of Rabbi Shimon Bar Yohai, a community of kabbalists gathered. In particular, during the 1560s and 1570s Moses Cordovero and Isaac Luria created new syntheses of the various strands in Kabbalah.

In particular, Luria—who became known as the *Ari,* the Lion, a Hebrew acronym for "the divine Rabbi Isaac"[36]— taught that creation began not with emanation from God, but with God's own withdrawal (which in Hebrew was called *tzimtzum*) in order to make a "space" for the creation of the universe. This occurred before the first words of Genesis; it was only after the *tzimtzum* that God's infinitude, called the *Ein Sof*-Infinite, was limited so that God could create "the heaven and the earth." Into that space God emanated the light of creation that, after much filtering and lowering of frequency, eventually congealed into the material universe we live in. Yet there is a notion that the imperfection of the world is due to an imperfection in the process of creation. While we are separate from the infinitude of God, God's essence is present in everything in our universe, for God is what animates it all. Embedded within the physical plane are hidden sparks of divinity, and our task in this life is *tikkun olam*-repair of the world, which is accomplished by righteous deeds that release and reunite these sparks to the *Ein Sof*-Infinite.

In the Ari's generation, with the Jewish people suffering from the trauma of the Spanish Expulsion and Inquisition, the Ari's teachings explained not only why the Messiah hadn't come (the divine sparks were trapped in the material world), but opened up an activist dimension to life by claiming that if one lived a more perfect, pure, and holy life, this would help repair the universe and bring the Messiah. As a result, kabbalistic beliefs and practices gained widespread popularity throughout the Jewish world not only as a way to purify oneself, but as a path for redemption of the Jewish people as a whole.

These mystical impulses found such fertile ground that by the mid-seventeenth century the Jewish world was swept up by a mystical fervor embodied in the movement that formed around Shabbetai Zevi, who proclaimed himself as The Messiah. After a few years of intensive activity, Shabbetai Zevi converted to Islam when threatened with death by the Ottoman Sultan. The grave danger to Jewish society and social structure posed by this mix of mysticism and messianism became clear. The resulting backlash repressed kabbalistic mysticism throughout the Jewish world; kabbalists refocused their efforts on the aspects of prayer, meditation, and theosophy rather than messianic activity.

Nevertheless, an undercurrent of mystical tradition stayed alive. Among *Mizrahi*-Oriental Jewry practices related to the <u>*Zohar*</u>-Brightness and Lurianic Kabbalah have continued in various forms until today, especially in Israel. In Eastern Europe, Kabbalah was reinvigorated by the Hasidic movement, which began in the mid-eighteenth century and continues to our day. Hasidism popularized the previously esoteric kabbalistic concepts in its teachings. The movement's popularity lay in its emphasis on ethical principles as a path toward holiness, particularly on the joy of living. Purity of intent together with the love of God and other humans was more important than learning, which made mystical ecstasy accessible to all classes of people. Music, dance, and storytelling were primary expressions of Hasidic observance. Much of current kabbalistic lore and practice popular in America today is based on the wide variety of Hasidic teachings, in part because they are precursors to modern psychological ways of understanding the self.

Despite this long past, most people in our generation, Jews and non-Jews, are unaware of the Kabbalah. The reason is that, during the last two centuries, the modern world and modern Judaism was particularly eager to reject and repress mysticism in favor of modern, enlightened thinking. In Western Europe and America this tradition was largely lost as Jews were emancipated in the nineteenth century, given equal citizenship, and enthusiastically integrated into an increasingly secular society. Abandoning the "primitive," "medieval," and "superstitious" aspects of Judaism was key to acceptance and prosperity in the modern world, and became reflected in the theology of Reform, Conservative, and Modern Orthodox Jewry.

In Eastern Europe modernization was slower, mirroring the less industrialized societies in which the Jews lived, especially Poland, Russia, and the Austro-Hungarian Empire which were the heartland of the Hasidic movement. Nevertheless, the twentieth century has seen their destruction. In Russia, the Russian Revolution largely stamped out all religion. In the rest of Eastern Europe, virtually all Jewish communities were destroyed by the Holocaust; the six million Jews murdered by the Nazis included at least one and a half million Hasidim, destroying those communities.

Among the Jews of North Africa and the Middle East, mystical traditions also survived due to the slower pace of modernization and secularization in their societies. However, after the establishment of the State of Israel in 1948, anti-Jewish violence erupted in these regions and virtually all the Jews emigrated with the next decade, mostly to Israel or France. Part of the acculturation process in these new countries was to jettison the mystical for the modern in order to be accepted and successful, an accelerated version of the nineteenth century emancipation process experienced by Western Jewry.

The two major Jewish communities of the second half of the twentieth century, the United States and Israel, have been overwhelmingly secular. Nevertheless, these two flourishing centers are providing fertile ground for Jewish spirituality and mysticism.

The Contemporary Kabbalistic Revival

Despite the modern decline of Kabbalah, today this "hidden spark" of Judaism is once again being revived, no doubt because the mystical experience at the heart of every religion reflects a primal human yearning. We are not satisfied by hearing the stories of other's encounters with the divine; we want a taste for ourselves. In our time this is reflected in a renewed interest in Jewish prayer practices, meditation, chanting, song, ritual items, and amulets.

The events of the Holocaust and the State of Israel have led many Jews to wonder about whether there is a deeper mystical significance to the survival of the Jews and the revival of Jewish political sovereignty. At the same time there is an increasing awareness of the oneness of all, of the "invisible lines of connection" (to use the phrase of Rabbi Lawrence Kushner) that connects each of us to all creation.[37] The growing ecological crisis and our increasing ecological awareness is teaching us again that we are indivisible from all of creation. The most important prayer in Judaism, known as the *Shma*-listen, declares the unity of all creation in the face of our surface perception of multiplicity: "Listen Israel: YHVH is our God, YHVH is One." This knowledge that what we do—or don't do—impacts all of creation in ways we may never know gives us a responsibility for *tikkun olam*-repair of the world, and for *tsedek*-justice, the pursuit of right living and justice in the world.

Today's kabbalistic revival is being nourished by a number of sources, especially the following:

- ASHKENAZI-*EUROPEAN ORTHODOX TRADITIONS*—The surviving communities of Hasidic Jews have maintained a living kabbalistic practice in the framework of Orthodox Jewish observance. Among the best known is Habad (Lubavitch), who have made a special effort at outreach to nonorthodox Jews worldwide.

- MIZRAHI-*ORIENTAL ORTHODOX TRADITIONS*—Especially in Israel there is a reinvigoration of the religious and mystical traditions of *Mizrahi*-Oriental Jewry, partly as a reaction to the modern and secular aspects of Israeli society that are perceived as antithetical to the culture of *Mizrahi*-Oriental Jews.

- *ACADEMIC SCHOLARSHIP*—The modern academic study of Kabbalah was founded early in the twentieth century by Professor Gershom Scholem. It is primarily focused on analysis of kabbalistic texts, largely from the medieval and early modern periods, providing insights into the worldview of those kabbalists, and the influence of Kabbalah on Judaism as a whole. In general this literature, focused on the past, is cautious about speculating how these ideas and practices might have a life today.

- *JEWISH RENEWAL*—A "post-denominational" movement, it was founded mainly by Rabbi Zalman Schachter-Shalomi and Rabbi Shlomo Carlbach *(z"l)*, whose lineage is from the Habad Hasidim. The aim is to revive kabbalistic views and practices in a nonorthodox way that remains permeable to the cross-cultural influences in modern life.

- *FEMINISM*—As in Jewish life in general, women and the feminist movement have been among the most dynamic factors in the contemporary evolution of Kabbalah. While it is true that virtually all earlier kabbalists were men and traditional kabbalistic literature, like Rabbinic literature in general, assumes a patriarchal view of the world, many contemporary feminists are reclaiming and reusing these symbols in a more egalitarian fashion. In particular, the kabbalistic images of *Shekhinah*-Presence as the female aspect of God and of *Binah*-Understanding as the cosmic mother are being utilized in new ritual and liturgy that is gender inclusive and affirmative of the feminine dimension of God's creation.

Non-Jewish Mystical Traditions

> Abraham willed all that he owned to Isaac; but to Abraham's
> sons by concubines Abraham gave gifts while he was still liv-
> ing, and he sent them away from his son Isaac eastward, to
> the land of the East. (Genesis 25:5–6)

Today many Jews have searched, and found, spiritual fulfill-
ment in the paths of other religious and cultural traditions.
This is part of the process of the globalization of culture, the
permeability of traditions that exist today. The response to
this phenomenon varies among contemporary kabbalists.
Some believe that Jews need not look elsewhere for spiritual
development because it all exists within Judaism—although
it may have been neglected or hidden in the last generations. Others believe that cross-fertilization between religious traditions is not only inevitable, but has always
happened and can be positive when handled consciously.

In his recent conversations with Jewish leaders, during
which the similarities and differences between Judaism and
Tibetan Buddhism were explored, the Dalai Lama chal-
lenged them to make the Jewish mystical traditions more
well-known among their own people.[38] Many people have
remarked on the similarities between various Jewish practices and doctrines, and those of other religions, such as
meditation or astrology. The _Zohar_-Brightness itself makes
the following commentary:

Rabbi Abba said: One day I came to a city of the people of the East, and they told me some wisdom that they had inherited from ancient times. They also had books explaining this wisdom, and they brought me one such book

In this book it was written that when a person meditates in this world, a spirit is transmitted to him from on high....

In that book I found all the rites and practices involved in the worship of the stars and constellations....

All these books can confuse a person. This is because the people of the East were great sages, who inherited this wisdom from Abraham. He had given it to the sons of his concubines. (_Zohar_ 1:99b)[39]

From this we can deduce that Jewish mystics have long known of other mystical traditions and have a certain respect for their power and truth. This also reveals their traditional Judeo-centric perspective (no different, in this sense, than most other traditions), in that they see the traditions of "the East" as deriving from Abraham, but have become misguided. This parallels the traditional attribution of the _Sefer Yetzirah_-Book of Formation, the kabbalistic text upon which much Jewish meditative and astrological practices are based, to Abraham, which was passed on through the lineage of Isaac. Yet there are also hints in the Bible of another Jewish perspective that is more respectful of differences:

For let all people walk everyone in the name of his god, and we will walk in the name of YHVH our God for ever and ever. (Micah 4:5)

From our perspective today it is harder to be certain about which direction influences flowed in—from Judaism to other religions, other religions into Judaism or both—or whether similar practices evolved independently in response to similar human conditions. Being open to dialogue concerning the experiences of other religious traditions is more typical of today's non-Orthodox Jewish kabbalists.

Non-Jewish Kabbalah

Today Kabbalah is being revealed to the world along with the spiritual traditions of many other people, and is available to those who wish to learn from it. What is unique about Kabbalah is that it has already had a long history and influence in the non-Jewish world.

About 500 years ago, during the European Renaissance, the Christian world discovered Kabbalah. In the fifteenth century Pico della Mirandola of Florence had a number of kabbalistic texts translated into Latin. He and others speculated that they had rediscovered lost ancient knowledge that would make it possible to understand Pythagoras, Plato, and other ancients, as well as the secrets of the Catholic faith. Pico believed that "no science can better convince us of the divinity of Jesus Christ than magic and the Kabbalah."[40] This created quite a stir, and the Christian Kabbalah, which also drew on alchemical symbolism, developed for a few hundred years independently of Jewish Kabbalah.

While interest in the Christian Kabbalah faded out by the late eighteenth century, a new occult tradition was born in the early nineteenth century that saw in the Tarot cards (whose earliest existing examples are from the fifteenth century) a kabbalistic system of hidden knowledge. This tradition grew out of Christian Kabbalah, but combined it with various other esoteric speculations related to alchemy and astrology. As developed in France by Levi and Papus, and in England by the Golden Dawn school that included Waite and Crowley, this evolved into the philosophy and practice of Tarot that has come down to the present.

Some of the elements of Tarot card deck that are seen as links to Kabbalah include: the twenty-two Hebrew letters associated with the major arcana; the ten *sefirot*-emanations associated with the one through ten cards in each of the four suits of the minor arcana; the four worlds associated with the four suits and four face cards in each suit. Some people speculate that Tarot cards derived from an earlier kabbalistic system designed for meditation or divination, but there is no hard evidence.

The best way to think of the Tarot's tradition of Kabbalah (usually spelled Qabala or Cabala) in relation to the Jewish Kabbalah is as an independent offshoot of the Jewish mystical tradition. Tarot is a spiritual practice that contains kabbalistic elements and symbols that many people find to be a source of inspiration and guidance. Sometimes this is a first step to a deeper exploration of Jewish Kabbalah.

Nevertheless, there is no doubt that the predominant attitude of Jewish kabbalists toward the Christian Kabbalah and of modern academics toward the Tarot ranges between derision and amusement.[41] Fundamentally, they believe that separating kabbalistic symbols and speculations from their intrinsic connection to Jewish texts and practices leads to misunderstanding and misuse. In this, as in many other ways, within the culture of the West the Jews were the first and archetypal "other," whose cultural artifacts were appropriated at will by the dominant culture. This is quite similar to the attitude of many indigenous people today toward the casual appropriation of symbols from their spiritual traditions.

Kabbalah's Place in Judaism

> Now all of the people were seeing the thunder-voices and
> the torches and the voice of the shofar and the mountain
> smoking; when the people saw, they fell back and stood far
> away. (Exodus 20:15)

The Mystical Torah

A fundamental aspect of every religion is the distinction
between the sacred and the profane, for it is the sacred dimension of existence that religion aims to address. In this sense,
the root source of every religion is a mystical experience. In
many religions this experience is thought to be possible at
any time and place. For others, especially the revealed religions, it may be focused on the memory of the experience of
a particular individual in a specific time and place that subsequently becomes a model for others. Some experience this as

primarily transcendent, others as primarily immanent. Nevertheless, the core experience of an encounter with a divine dimension is universal. The rites, ritual, and customs that evolve into a religion are human attempts to remember, recover, and invoke those experiences of awe and wonder. It is the mystical dimension of every religious tradition that keeps the religion alive, finding the inner spark hidden under the garments of tradition, seeking to recreate, re-experience, and relive those experiences *now*, and by *us*, rather than only remembering the experiences of those who came before.

Judaism is a revealed religion: it began with God speaking to Abraham and reached its peak with the revelation at Mount Sinai, where the whole Jewish people perceived the Ten Commandments spoken by God. The Torah's report of the revelation at Mount Sinai was of an overwhelming experience of synesthesia, of "seeing the thunder-voices." This expresses a sensory experience beyond the normal division of the five senses, a confusion or mixing of our normal divisions between the senses, or an overflow of experience that superactivates all the senses, merging them together. This type of mystical experience can be frightening; perhaps that is why the people moved away from the mountain and asked Moses to be their intermediary.

The rest of the Torah is considered God's word as revealed through Moses. The Torah scroll kept in the synagogue, where it is read out publicly to the congregation throughout the year, includes the "Five Books of Moses" that form the first part of the Bible. In addition to the Torah, the Jewish Bible includes the Prophets (such as Isaiah, Ezekiel, and others) and the Writings (such books as Song of Songs, Psalms, Ruth, Esther, etc.), which are also considered to be divinely inspired sacred texts.

Much of the structure of subsequent Jewish thought developed in the form of commentary on the revealed texts because it was presumed that all knowledge had been revealed in the holy scriptures. Our task was, and is, to interpret the texts properly in order to understand them for each age. The term "Torah" evolved to refer not only to the first five biblical books, but to refer generally to all Jewish commentary and study. This is true for *halacha*-Jewish law (*halacha* literally means "the way"), and it is also true for other aspects of Judaism, including Kabbalah.

The danger inherent in writing things down is that they become venerated as "the truth" rather than "a truth." Over time they have a tendency to become hardened and unresponsive to changing conditions. Thus, the Rabbinic tradition believes that, in addition to the written Torah given to Moses, an oral Torah was also transmitted; an oral tradition that tells us how to understand and interpret the written Torah. In Judaism, fundamentalism is out of place; the written Torah must be viewed via the lens of the oral Torah guiding interpretation and understanding. This perspective provided some latitude for the ancient Rabbis as new interpretations of the ancient texts were introduced. Over time this oral Torah was recorded as the Talmud, a process that took many generations and was usually written down only when there was a danger of it being forgotten. Subsequently, the Talmud itself became venerated as a holy text, revealing how to interpret and understand the original Torah. *Halacha*-Jewish law inevitably became the source and focus for much legal casuistry, for over time one has to become ever more clever to fit the received "law" into new circumstances. Layer upon layer of interpretations were laid down, like silt in a riverbed. The law develops and God's word—and God—are experienced as ever more other and distant.

The mystical impulse is to collapse this distance and cut through the layers of legalism—like a flash flood scours a riverbed—in order to experience God's immanence. What is special about Judaism is that kabbalists did not deny the legitimacy of the oral Torah's teachings and methodology. Rather than going around or outside of the legal tradition, the kabbalists went *through* it, developing Kabbalah in the context of the Rabbinic tradition of Biblical and Talmudic study. Like a flash flood, their goal was to cleanse, revive, and—inevitably—redirect the flow of Judaism. Historically, many of the greatest Jewish minds were at once both legal scholars and kabbalists. It has not always been an either/or situation, but rather a question of degree and emphasis. Over the centuries of Jewish life there has been an ebb and flow in emphasis and popularity between the rationalist and mystical impulses, with the rationalists focusing on theological and legal discourse while the mystics concentrate on either the theosophical inner life of God or on *hokhmah penimit*-inner wisdom, the ecstatic personal spiritual experience.

While *halacha*-Jewish law is the logical head of Judaism, Kabbalah is the mystical heart. Kabbalah's intuitive perception of oneness balances the fine divisions and logic of the law. Kabbalah is not something separate, but evolved as an intrinsic and inseparable part of Judaism. While some kabbalistic practices have evolved in addition to the generally accepted practices of Jewish observance, much of Kabbalah involves a way of seeing and understanding the sacred dimension of traditional Jewish rituals.

Kabbalistic Methods of Torah Interpretation

> Woe to the wicked
> who say that Torah is merely a story!
> They look at this garment and no further.
> Happy are the righteous
> who look at Torah properly!

> As wine must sit in a jar,
> so Torah must sit in this garment.
> So look only at what is under the garment!
> So all those words and all those stories—
> they are garments! (*Zohar* 3:152a)[42]

For both rationalists and mystics, the lens of Jewish self-understanding has been the Bible and its interpretation. Thus, many of the great kabbalistic texts, like the _Zohar_-Brightness are presented as commentaries on the Bible. Like the legalists, the kabbalists have always claimed that their traditions began with Moses (some claim Abraham) and have been orally passed down over the centuries. Also like the legalists, the kabbalists presume that the Torah itself is the revealed word of God, but our understanding is incomplete due to our own limitations. Our understanding is constantly evolving as we ourselves grow and change, and the task of the kabbalist is to unfold the hidden layers of meaning locked in the sacred texts, waiting to be revealed to the worthy student. The Torah is not to be understood literally, but symbolically; the kabbalists were those who studied and invented ways to understand this symbolism and its deeper truths. The kabbalists' goal was not to overcome Judaism, but to discover and reveal its inner secrets. The Torah is seen not merely as the law of the Jewish people; it reveals the inner secrets of God and the universe.

Naming God

The Talmud relates that there is a heavenly Torah written with "black fire on white fire" that has existed since before our universe was created, and that it was the template for that creation. Our earthly Torah is merely a manifestation in this world of the heavenly Torah, and the kabbalists believe that the apparently blank white areas of the Torah contain as much hidden meaning as the black letters.

In this way, many techniques were developed to infuse new meanings into ancient holy texts. For example, kabbalists believe that the reason the Torah scroll does not contain Hebrew vowel-points is so that alternate readings and pronunciation of the text are possible, resulting in different interpretations.[43] There is even a tradition that the Torah originally had no spaces at all between the letters, so it formed one continuous Name of God, the template of God's unfolding in the universe.

God is referred to by many names in the Bible, and the many words used in English reflect this variety: Lord, God, Almighty, Place, God Most High, Provider, and others. For Jews, however, the most holy name of God is the four letter name—יהוה, transliterated here as YHVH, which is referred to by Jews as *Hashem*-The Name, and in English as "the Tetragrammaton." When *YHVH*-The Name appears in the Bible or *siddur*-prayerbook, Jews traditionally pronounce another of the names of God, usually "*Adonai*-My Lord." Non-Jewish biblical interpreters sometimes pronounce *YHVH*-The Name as Jehovah or Yahweh, but to the Jewish mind—and considerable scholarship—these are misreadings, for the *YHVH*-The Name is unpronounceable.

YHVH-The Name conveys the sense of God as a verb, as

Being/Becoming. The letters are related to the root of the verb "to be," but a tense cannot be attributed. Past, present, and future are all included, implying that God is/was/will be, meaning that God exists in a realm beyond the dimension of time. This also implies that God is the one who brings Being into existence. The *Zohar*-Brightness points out the connection between *YHVH*-The Name and the name given to Moses at the burning bush, which derives from the same verb root: אהיה אשר אהיה *Ehyeh-Asher-Ehyeh* (Exodus 3:14), means "I will be what I will be." Pure Being, uncontrollable, beyond time.[44]

The *Shema*—or, a Word about Our Sponsor

YHVH-The Name (יהוה) appears twice in the *Shema*-Listen prayer, which is the most important prayer in Judaism. The *Shema*-Listen is recited three times a day, and is inscribed in Jewish amulets (see section on Amulets page 95). Ever since Rabbi Akiva died saying the *Shema*-Listen while being tortured by the Romans, it has been taught that the *Shema*-Listen should be the last words uttered in this life. Said to be the sum of Jewish belief, the *Shema*-Listen is usually translated as:

> Hear, O Israel: the Lord is our God, the Lord is one.
> (Deuteronomy 6:4)

When translated word for word it goes like this:

שמע	*Shema*-Listen
ישראל	*Yisrael*-Israel
יהוה	*YHVH*-The Name
אלהינו	*Elohyenu*-Our God
יהוה	*YHVH*-The Name
אחד	*Ekhad*-One

A more recent translation emphasizes the context of the sentence in the Torah, where Moses is speaking to the Israelite people in the desert, emphasizing their adherence to their God and not to other gods:

Hear, O Israel! The Lord is our God, the Lord alone. *(Tanakh)*[45]

Every translation is an interpretation, and kabbalists are masters of constant reinterpretation. Kabbalists understand *Elohim* (*Eloheynu* means "our *Elohim*") as the name of God, which refers to the manifestation of definitions and distinctions; it is this mode of God that is the creator described in Genesis 1. Kabbalists believe that the creation of the material, perceptual universe that we dwell in required that God's endless infinitude be limited, resulting in the world of distinctions. This is the world of duality that we perceive around us, the dialectical world of either/or.

YHVH-The Name (יהוה) appears twice in the *Shema*-Listen, and is the focus of the prayer. For kabbalists, this name of

God refers to the unity of the Creator and creation. Kabbalists are certain that the multiple stages of Being/Becoming represented by the Tree-of-Life are ultimately one and united, for "*YHVH*-The Name is One." Paradoxes are due to our own perceptual limitations that are mired in the world of distinctions. While we perceive the world as "either/or," from God's perspective things are really "both/and." This is the monotheism of Kabbalah. The *Shema*-Listen witnesses and affirms the essential unity of all manifestations of creation, crying out for us to really listen. Along these lines, two contemporary feminist writers have reinterpreted the *Shema*-Listen as follows:

> Hear, O Israel—The divine abounds everywhere and
> dwells in everything; the many are One.
>
> MARCIA FALK[46]

> Shema, be attentive to this!
> Yisrael, you who walk the Spiritpath
> Shekinah, the Being One,
> Elohanu, All Spirits,
> Shekinah, the Being One,
> Echad, embraces all being.
>
> LYNN GOTTLIEB[47]

Some modern kabbalists have interpreted the paragraph that follows the *Shema*-Listen (see section on Amulets, page 95) as an instruction for meditation, and use the *Shema*-Listen as a phrase to be repeated in meditation, like a mantra.

Gematria—Kabbalistic Numerology

One of the widely used methods of uncovering hidden meanings of the Torah is numerology based on Hebrew letters called *gematria*-numerology. The word itself is from Greek (related to "geometry"), indicating that the practice was borrowed from surrounding cultures where number mysticism was widespread, probably during the period of the Second Temple.

The recent interest in "bible codes" is an updated form of *gematria*-numerology, which shares the notion that secret messages are embedded in the text, truths beyond our normal understanding. It is interesting, however, that the traditional logic is inverted today: while *gematria*-numerology was meaningful for the ancient and medieval person of faith because the text was assumed to be of divine origin, today *gematria*-numerology is used to prove the divine origin of the text and, indirectly, the existence of God! Finding hidden connections proves both the accuracy of the text and the truth of the message uncovered by the interpreter, legitimizing as sacred both the text and the message.

Gematria-numerology assumes that each letter of the Hebrew alphabet represents a numerical value (see Table 1: The Hebrew Alphabet). By converting the letters of words or phrases into numerical values, one may discover that different words or phrases are "equivalent" and have a hidden connection. While this was considered one of the standard rules for interpreting Torah from at least Talmudic times, the kabbalistic interest in the hidden dimensions of the Torah leads to a special interest in *gematria*-numerology. Unlike Pythagorean and other numerological systems, in *gematria*-numerology the numbers themselves have no significance themselves other than as links between words of the Torah.

An example of how kabbalists apply these interpretive methods is to look at the last and first letter of Torah, ל-*lamed* and ב-*bet*, which form the word *lev*-heart. The *Zohar*-Brightness concludes from this that the study of Torah depends on the heart. It is the last and first letter, rather than the first and last, because one must continuously reread the Torah, and immediately upon finishing it start again, as is done on the holiday of *Simchat Torah*-Rejoicing in the Torah. Also, the ל-*lamed* and ב-*bet* are the only letters that can be combined with each of the letters of *YHVH*-The Name to form meaningful words. This is taken to mean that the heart is the place of direct connection to *YHVH*-The Name.[48] The *gematria*-numerology value of *lev*-heart is thirty-two, which refers to the "thirty-two mystical paths of wisdom" referred to in the opening of the *Sefer Yezirah*-Book of Formation, which are the twenty-two letters and ten *sefirot*-emanations of the Tree-of-Life.

In addition to the simple system of converting words to numbers and finding equivalencies, there are many other increasingly complex systems that describe between nine and seventy-two different forms of *gematria*-numerology! One of the more ancient systems is called *atbash*, which is a cipher substituting in reverse order the letters of the Hebrew alphabet: the last for the first, *tav* for *aleph*; the second to last for the second, *shin* for *bet*; etc. (this spells "a-t-b-sh"). This form is so ancient that it actually appears in the Biblical book of Jeremiah.[49]

The computer can be a useful contemporary tool for in *gematria*-numerology calculations, and programs such as *Gematrilator: The Gematria Calculator* (Davka Corporation) can help with this. It can be interesting to figure out the *gematria*-numerology of your name (Hebrew name, if you have one) and see any equivalencies with Biblical words or phrases.

The Torah of the Moment

The mystical impulse that enlivens Judaism is reflected in the Talmudic teaching that all Jews, in every generation, were present at the revelation at Mount Sinai, where God stated the Ten Commandments for all to hear. Of course, Moses and other prophets had their own personal revelations that they shared with the people as a whole, but the founding experience of the Jewish religion was in the public revelation at Sinai where all were present, and where it was available to all.

This is part of a fundamentally democratic, participatory

impulse in Judaism. While mystical practices and principles were usually taught only to those schooled in the Rabbinic tradition, it was known that mystical experiences were the heritage of all and potentially available to everyone. Indeed, the kabbalists believe that there is a unique interpretation of Torah available to each person, whose path to revelation will be their own.[50]

But the experience of Sinai is not only beyond class; it is also beyond time, for if we all were present at Sinai, that also means that Sinai is present for all of us *now*, if we only listen. That is, revelation is possible at every moment, for God's work of creation is not over and done with, but constant and continuous. In the mystic mind, time does not exist as a stone barrier, but as a silken veil.

The Structure of Reality, the Life of the Soul

The Four Worlds

> The existence stemming from God, extending to the lowest point, is divided into four divisions. (Rabbi Moses Cordovero, _Or Ne'erav_)[51]

Kabbalists developed a complex set of ideas concerning the structure of reality, its relationship to consciousness and the life of the soul. This multidimensional theory describing a multidimensional reality has come to be called the doctrine of "The Four Worlds," in the sense of different realms or universes. These are not distinct physical worlds, but interpenetrating realities that exist simultaneously; some kabbalists describe them as concentric, one within the other. In ascending order of spirituality these are known as _Assiyah-_

Making, *Yetzirah*-Formation, *Briyah*-Creation, and *Atzilut*-Nearness. These names are derived from Isaiah (43:7), which reads: "All who are called in My name, for my glory have I created, formed and made." There is a temporal hierarchy here in the sense that the creation of the universe was sequential: it began in the realm of *Atzilut*-Nearness, (named for its closeness to God), the most spiritual realm that is the location of the primordial Tree-of-Life, and was completed with *Assiyah*-Making, the physical realm of our daily existence. Since creation all four worlds exist simultaneously, intersect, and interpenetrate.

This doctrine has proved very fertile within Kabbalah up to our own time, and it has been used to organize many aspects of experience. All of these "fours" are related to the primordial source of these patterns, the four letter name of God, *YHVH*-The Name. See Table 3: Associations of the Four Worlds, which lists many of these associations.

While the *sefirot*-emanations of the Tree-of-Life came into existence in the world of *Atzilut*-Nearness, they are thought to be active in all four worlds as appropriate to the functioning of that world. Thus, the primordial pattern of the Tree-of-Life echoes through the worlds, and it is possible to speak of a Tree-of-Life in each world, just as kabbalists speak of a Tree-of-Life within each *sefirah*-emanation of the Tree-of-Life.

As can be seen from Table 3, some aspects of each of the four worlds are present to us always, such as the four

TABLE 3: ASSOCIATIONS OF THE FOUR WORLDS[52]

LETTER OF TETRAGRAMMATON	ה
LETTER-NAME	hey
WORLD	עשייה
WORLD TRANSLITERATION	Assiyah
WORLD (TRANSLATION)	Making, Action, Doing
REALM OF CONSCIOUSNESS	Physical; Action; Body
EXPERIENCE	Physical
MANIFESTATION	Doing
ELEMENT	Earth
MATTER STATE	Solid
IDENTITY	I-It
CONTENT	Shade of the Physical
SOUL	Vitality
SOUL: TRANSPERSONAL PSYCHOLOGY	Bioenergetic Field
LEVEL OF SOUL	*Nefesh*-Animation
SEFIROT-EMANATIONS (TRIADS)	*Shekhinah*
BODY	Feet or Base of the Spine
ANGELS	Raphael
DIRECTION	West
ANIMAL (EZEKIEL)	Bull
JUNGIAN PERSONALITY TYPES	Sensation
LEVEL OF CREATION	Completion
ANGELIC INHABITANTS	Ophanim
SEFIROT-EMANATIONS (FLOW OF CREATION)	Shekhinah
TORAH INTERPRETATION	*P'shat*-Simple (Surface)
COLOR (EXODUS 26:1)	Scarlet
BREATH	Exhale
NATURAL KINGDOM	Mineral
TAROT SUIT	Disks

ו	ה	י
vav	hey	yod
יצירה	בריאה	אצילות
Yetzirah	Briyah	Atzilut
Formation	Creation	Nearness, Emanation
Emotional; Feeling	Mental; Mind; Thought	Spiritual Being; Essence
Emotional	Mental	Spiritual
Feeling	Knowing	Essence-Being
Water	Air	Fire
Liquid	Gas	Plasma
I-Thou	S/He-Me	I Am That I Am
Angels	The Throne	*Sefirot*-Emanations
Emotion	Intellect	Uniqueness
Emotional Energy Field; Personal Self	Transpersonal Self; Higher Mind	Transcendental Field of Light; Oneness; Spirit
Ruach-Spirit	*Neshamah*-Breath	*Chayah*-Living Essence & *Yehidah*-Unity
Netzah-Hod-Yesod	Hesed-Gevurah-Tiferet	Keter-Hokhmah-Binah
Pelvis/Kidneys/Genitals	Lungs/Heart	Head
Uriel	Gabriel	Michael
East	North	South
Lion	Eagle	Human
Feeling	Thinking	Intuition
Something from Something	Something from Nothing	Nothingness
Chayot/Cherubim	Serafim	Sefirot/Partzufim
Next Six	Binah	Keter/Hokhmah
Remez-Hint (Deductive)	*Drash*-Expound (Metaphor)	*Sod*-Secret (Mystical)
Purple	Blue	White
Full Lungs	Inhale	Empty Lungs
Plant	Animal	Human
Cups	Swords	Wands

dimensions of experience: physical, emotional, mental, spiritual. On the other hand, some aspects are more obscure, such as the levels of the soul or the realms of the angels, throne, and *sefirot*-emanations. Some kabbalistic practices of prayer and meditation were aimed at making it possible to experience these other worlds; indeed, that was part of the intent of the practices of both the *ma'aseh merkavah*-Workings of the Chariot school and Abulafian meditation.

Five Levels of the Soul

The human soul is thought to exist simultaneously in each of the four worlds. However, the soul's manifestation in each world, and connection to it, is given a different name.

For the kabbalist, physicality does not exist in and of itself; physical existence is animated by God, whose emanation is everflowing, and without whom all physical existence would collapse in a moment.

The first level, *Nefesh*-Animation, is the soul level of the physical world of *Assiyah*-Making; every physically existing thing, from an atom to a planet has a *Nefesh*-Animation that animates its existence. For humans, the experience on the level of *Nefesh*-Animation is in the realm of the bodily senses that involve physicality and movement. It is at the level of *Nefesh*-Animation that the physical, electromagnetic, and biomechanical energy interfaces with and is part of the energy flow of the world at large. Physical training and movements that attune us to this realm include such practices as yoga and tai chi.

The second level, *Ruach*-Spirit, means both wind and spirit. It is associated with basic consciousness and emotional awareness. This is the location of our spiritual life, which is formed by life experience, spiritual practices, and our relationship with others. This level of reality is considered more characteristically human than the *Nefesh*-Animation, and the development of our *Ruach*-Spirit soul level is considered much more important to our personal development. The Biblical prophets attained the highest level of consciousness possible on this level, called *ruach ha-kodesh*-holy spirit.

One of the first blessings recited upon rising in the morning is a prayer of thanks: "My God, the *neshamah* you placed in me is pure." God has given us the opportunity to reach this third level of the soul, which is directly connected to the Source of Life. Its name, *Neshamah*, derives from the word for breath; it was with this same divine breath that the first Adam became a living being. This level of the soul is connected to the world of *Briyah*-Creation, which is the realm of the heavenly throne, also known as the heavenly chariot. In human experience this is the mental realm of thoughts, ideas, abstractions, and the ability to speak them.

For kabbalists this faculty of speech is what distinguishes

humans from other creatures; yet, while we have the ability to cultivate this soul level, this is not inborn like the levels of *Nefesh*-Animation and *Ruach*-Spirit. Our soul growth on the *Neshamah*-Breath level is achieved through the pursuit of righteousness, which is asserted to be the purpose of our life.

Concerning these three levels of the soul, the *Zohar*-Brightness comments:

> The *Nefesh*-Animation is the lowest stimulus. It is close to the body and nourishes it. The body depends upon it, and it depends upon the body. After this it is prepared, and becomes a throne upon which the *Ruach*-Spirit may rest, through the stimulus of the *Nefesh*-Animation, which depends upon the body, as it is written "so that the *Ruach*-Spirit may be poured upon us from on high" (Isaiah 32:15). Once they have both been prepared, they are ready to receive the *Neshamah*-Breath, for the *Ruach*-Spirit becomes a throne for the *Neshamah*-Breath to rest upon...And they are near to one another: the *Nefesh*-Animation is near to the *Ruach*-Spirit, and the *Ruach*-Spirit is near to the *Neshamah*-Breath, and all is one. (*Zohar* I, 205b–206a)[53]

The fourth level of the soul, which exists in the world of *Atzilut*-Nearness, is *Chayah*-Living Essence, which is related to the Hebrew word for life. This is the level beyond language; it is our constant connection to the source of life, pure being. Experiencing this level of the soul is the goal of many kabbalistic meditative practices; it is an altered state of consciousness. The rare human who reaches this level of

God-consciousness experiences a merging with God, which is called *devekut*-adherence, and, as mystics of many traditions will say, is beyond words.

There is also thought to be a fifth level of the soul, *Yehidah*-Unity, which points beyond the four worlds back to the primordial source, the *Ein Sof*-Infinite that exists beyond and prior to the realm of the creation. While the four letters of the *YHVH*-The Name are associated with the four lower levels of the soul, the *Yehidah*-Unity is said to be the tip of the *yod-*ʼ, which points to its source in the *Ein Sof*-Infinite. This is the spark of pure God-essence that connects us to the source of all creation, to the cosmic seed; it is the part of us that is God—it is both a part of us and a part of God. It is the level of the soul that maintains a connection to the oneness of God prior to the duality of creation.

Transmigration of Souls

As can be seen, kabbalistic doctrine asserts that there are multiple levels of soul for each person. The logical conclusion is that the soul exists both before and after the life of the body, and that there is a process called *gilgul*-reincarnation. The belief in *gilgul*-reincarnation became commonplace among kabbalists by about the thirteenth century. There are notions that both good and evil souls reincarnate: evil souls as a punishment until they purify themselves by fixing what they have done wrong, and good souls in order to assist in *tikkun olam*-repair of the world.

Jewish death rituals include the cleansing of the body, which is wrapped in a simple shroud and then placed in a pine coffin, and swift burial within about forty-eight hours. There is a special prayer, the *kaddish*-sanctification, that is said for the dead at burial, then regularly for the next eleven months. All of these rituals are aimed at easing the departure of the soul from the body, as well as toward the welfare of the surviving family members. It is thought that during the first week of death the soul is confused, and wanders between the grave and home. During this week, called "sitting *shiva*-seven," the surviving family is in mourning; they stay home and are consoled by friends. It is thought that this will help the dead person's spirit understand that its body has died and that it needs to move on. Some Jewish doctrine asserts that without a complete body the soul will have difficulty moving on, which is why Jewish tradition objects to cremation.

The Ari developed the notion that all souls are related to sparks from the soul of the *Adam Kadmon*-Primordial Human, which were scattered with the first sin. The purpose of *gilgul*-reincarnation is to reconstitute the soul structure of this primal soul, which is why our task in life is to raise the sparks back to their rightful place in the cosmos. Sparks from different parts of the body of *Adam Kadmon*-Primordial

Human have different qualities; each individual may be made up of multiple soul sparks, and, in this way, be related to the souls of multiple people in the past and in the current generation. Some kabbalistic literature traces how various Biblical or Talmudic characters are reincarnations of prior figures, explaining later lives in context of their former lives. Part of the charisma of kabbalistic leaders such as the Ari and the Ba'al Shem Tov was their ability to identify the soul roots of their followers, connecting them with their prior lives and thereby helping them understand the path of their life in this *gilgul*-reincarnation.

In addition there is the notion that souls whose bodies have died can enter into the body of an already living person. This notion of *ibbur*-foreign soul was common even in the Talmudic era, but by the sixteenth century came to refer to the soul of a righteous person, who may come back to perform a *tikkun*-repair for themselves or others. We have reports that the famous sixteenth century kabbalist and legal scholar, Rabbi Joseph Caro, channeled an *ibbur*-foreign soul, who taught him ways of interpreting Torah.

In contrast, the entry of an evil spirit came to be called a *dibbuk*-evil spirit at this time. The *dibbuk*-evil spirit was not allowed to reincarnate due to its sins in life, and therefore sought refuge in the living. Still, it was thought that it was sins on the part of a living person that allowed a *dibbuk*-evil spirit to enter the living body, and the services of a *ba'al shem*-master of The Name (see chapter below on "Kabbalistic Healing") needed to be engaged in order to exorcise the *dibbuk*-evil spirit by means of a *tikkun*-repair that would move the *dibbuk*-evil spirit onto the next stage of the soul's journey.

Angels and Demons

> Jacob left Beersheba and set out for Haran. He came upon a certain place and stopped there for the night. Taking one of the stones of that place, he put it under his head and lay down in that place. He had a dream; a ladder was set on the ground and its top reached the sky, and angels of God were going up and down on it. And God was standing beside him. (Genesis 28:10–13)

The Bible, of course, is full of angelic encounters, but the angels are not named individually. It is only in the post-Biblical literature that an extensive angelology develops, particularly with the *ma'aseh merkavah*-Workings of the Chariot literature, where there are various angelic inhabitants of the different levels of the Heavenly Halls. Angels are thought to be heavenly messengers, much like humans but without the free will of humans. Much contemporary literature has been influenced by the long development of the kabbalistic literature of angelology. This is reflected in angelic names which are almost all Hebrew and commonly use the suffixes *ya* or *el*, which mean "of God." The best known are the four archangels: Michael-Who Is Like God is the angel of mercy; Gabriel-Strength of God is the angel of fire and war; Uriel-Light of God is the angel of divine light; Raphael-Healer of God is the angel of healing.

Part of the reason the four archangels are so well known is that they are mentioned in the traditional Jewish bedtime prayers included in the Jewish *siddur*-prayerbook which are to be said just before falling asleep. The angel prayer calls upon these angels for protection during the night:

> In the name of YHVH-The Name, God of Israel: may Michael be at my right, Gabriel at my left, Uriel before me, Raphael behind me and above my head the *Shekhinah*-Presence of God.

Kabbalists believe that calling on the angels is our way to plug into the infinite resource of God's energy, the energy that maintains creation at every moment. Angels are like radio stations: they are always sending out their energy. We just need to be properly "tuned-in" in order to receive them clearly. Angels are seen as messengers between the heavenly and earthly realms; when we tune in we become conduits helping them do their work in the world.

Demons are thought to be spirit beings of a rank between angels and humans. They are the transmitters of negative energy; addictions are a good example of the kind of havoc they bring. They are not agents of God, and can therefore be rebuffed or even controlled by humans. In general, kabbalists have believed that demons are more numerous and have more power during the dark nighttime hours. This is one of the origins of the practice of *tikkun hatzot*-midnight prayers aimed at helping the world get through the darkest part of the daily cycle. Like angels, it is ultimately up to us whether we tune into the negative energy of the demonic.

Kabbalistic Healing: The Shamanic Dimension of Judaism

Moses made a copper serpent and mounted it on a pole;
and when anyone was bitten by a serpent, he would look at
the copper serpent and live. (Numbers 21:9)

Shamanism is the term used to describe the type of healing
practiced by many indigenous people throughout the world.
The shaman typically undergoes an initiation—either
planned or spontaneous—which includes a journey away
from the everyday world into the spirit world. The result of
this initiation is a unique knowledge and power of the hidden, spiritual dimension of the world that makes the shaman
able to serve as a healer to others in his or her community.

Judaism actually has an ancient shamanic tradition which
has continuously evolved with the mystical path of the

Kabbalah. Like many other aspects of Jewish mysticism, much of it was repressed and lost in the modern age, and is only recently being revived. Moses is perhaps the archetypal Jewish shaman. After his mystical encounter with God at the burning bush he becomes a direct channel to God. Not only does he perform various miracles to convince both Pharaoh and the Jewish people to leave Egypt, but he is able to perform mass healings.

Healing is the essential task of the shaman, and there is a long history of the development of the healing arts among Jews. This shamanic dimension of the healing arts is less well-known today among Jews, as among other western peoples, but we see vestiges of it in the modern image of the Jewish physician; indeed, since at least the Middle Ages Jews have constituted a high proportion of the medical profession relative to their numbers in the general population in Europe, North Africa, and the Middle East. Moses' copper snake is thought to be one of the sources of the caduceus as a symbol of the medical profession.

Ba'al Shem-Master of The Name

> So Moses cried out to *YHVH*-The Name, saying, "O God, pray heal her!" (Numbers 12:13)

In addition to physicians, who focused their methods on diet and botanical preparations, Jewish literature reports a number of other healing methods associated with shamanism. Physical ailments are thought to be only a manifestation on the physical level of an illness that is simultaneously taking place on other levels of the soul as well, and requires healing on those levels. Prayer has long been considered an important healing tool. Having others, particularly those who are spiritually pure—often called a *tzaddik*-righteous one—pray for the health of someone has been considered efficacious. This is institutionalized in the *shabbat*-sabbath prayer service. In the morning immediately after the reading of the Torah a prayer is recited by the congregation on behalf of those who are ill and need healing. Prayer is the Jewish version of the shaman's traveling between this world and the worlds of other spirits and demons. From the dance of King David before the holy ark to the swaying and chanting of Hasidim, ecstatic prayer is thought to bring one into alignment with the other spirit realms, and closer to God, as a means of gaining healing help on that level.

Often the prayers of Rabbis thought to be particularly saintly are solicited. Indeed, it is thought that the already dead are in a good position to intercede on our behalf, and both dead relatives and saintly Rabbis are appealed to for help. This is one of the reasons for the custom of visiting tombs, talking to the soul of the departed, and leaving notes of supplication. Particularly on the anniversary of a person's death—known by the Yiddish term *yahrzeit*-anniversary—

their soul is thought to return to their gravesite and come closest to our realm.

There is a long tradition of healers known as *ba'al shem*-master of The Name, a term used since at least the early Middle Ages. Sometimes these were Rabbis, but not necessarily. This term is best known today from the title *Ba'al Shem Tov*-Master of the Good Name given to Israel ben Eliezer, the founder of modern Hasidism who lived in the eighteenth century, and who was not a Rabbi. The title refers not to having a good reputation (although that may have been true as well), but to the ability to effect magical cures by virtue of knowledge of the name of God. Someone who was a *ba'al shem*-master of The Name was a mystic who possessed secret knowledge of the YHVH-The Name and other holy names of God, and could use this for performing miracles, especially healings. This field of "practical" or "applied" Kabbalah, in contrast to more theoretical or meditative trends, was common during the period of the Spanish Kabbalah, and combined prayers, incantations, and the writing of amulets. The roots of this magical tradition are older than the theoretical Kabbalah, beginning at least with the Talmud. From the sixteenth century onward the practice spread in central and eastern Europe, and became fused with folk healing, which included the preparation of medicinal remedies derived from plant, mineral, and animal matter.

This could also include the laying on of hands, a practice reported in the Talmud.

A *ba'al shem*-master of The Name was also the person turned to for exorcising evil spirits who had taken possession of a human body. In general their healing work was considered part of their service to the community. Many kabbalists warned about crossing the line into using Holy Names for private gain, a clear sign that such activity was taking place!

A related kabbalistic healing practice for a person that is near death is to change one's Hebrew (that is, "real") name via a ritual prayer contained in the prayer book, either by changing their name completely or by adding a name that alludes to life and health, such as *Chaim*-life or *Raphael*-God's healer. This practice, which has its roots in the Talmud, is thought to be effective because the Angel of Death performs its work by finding a person whose death has been decreed by the "court on high." Changing the person's name takes the form of a legal procedure, which "cheats" the Angel of Death by making it impossible to find the victim, a clear reflection of Kabbalah's emphasis on the power of words and speech.

One term that has crossed into English usage from the tradition of magical Kabbalah is "abracadabra," which is used in association with a magical incantation. This is the Hebrew phrase *abra-kadabra*, which means "I will create as I speak." The phrase contains the second word of the Torah, *bara*-create; the remaining letters of the phrase add up to twenty-six, the same as *YHVH*-The Name.[54] Thus, in speaking the incantation, the practical kabbalist is attempting to emulate the creation through speech of God.

Dreamwork

> And Joseph said to Pharaoh, "Pharaoh's dreams are one and the same: God has told Pharaoh what He is about to do." (Genesis 41:25)

Many cultures have thought that the spirit world communicates with humans through the medium of dreams. This view is assumed by kabbalistic doctrine, which takes dreams seriously. There are numerous reports of dreams resulting in certain legal decisions, of prophesying the future, and even of liturgical poetry being dictated to people through dreams. While positive dreams are often thought to be initiated by an angelic messenger, negative dreams are similarly thought to be caused by demonic spirits. The dead who have departed this world, particularly during the last year, are thought to contact us through dreams.

Within Judaism the skill of dream interpretation has been honored since biblical times, and many of the key stories of the Torah involve dreams. Joseph is seen as the archetypal master of the dream who is able to interpret his own and other's dreams as allegories of the future. He is very clear to attribute his prophetic gift to God, and sees himself as God's vehicle.

The Talmud also takes dreams seriously, and lays down the basic principle that "All dreams follow their interpretation."[55] That is to say, the Rabbis were aware of the psychological effects of interpretation, that an interpretation can become a self-fulfilling prophecy. Thus, the role of the interpreter can be crucial, and it was suggested that negative dreams not be divulged for fear of aiding in their manifestation. Nevertheless, many books were written to help with dream interpretation, and this art has been considered important and honorable.

Amulets

> Hear, O Israel: YHVH our God, YHVH is one. You shall love YHVH your God with all your heart, with all your soul and with all your might. These words, which I command you today, are to be upon your heart. You are to repeat them with your children and are to speak of them when your sit in your house, and when you walk in the way, when you lie down and when you get up. Bind them as a sign on your hand and as a symbol between your eyes. You shall write them upon the doorposts of your house and on your gates. (Deuteronomy 6:4-9)

The first line of this quote is known as the *Shema*-Listen, which is thought to encapsulate the sum of Jewish belief (see the chapter entitled "Kabbalah's Place in Judaism"). The paragraph that follows it tells us what to do: repeat it, teach it, tie it to our bodies, and write it on our houses. The last two practices have resulted in two amulets that have been in continuous use from ancient times until today: the *mezuzah*-doorpost scroll and *tefillin*-amulets.

What is unique about these Jewish amulets is that they always incorporate a piece of parchment with hand-written text from the Torah. Their purpose is to fulfill the commandment described in this passage, thereby reminding us of our connection to God and bringing blessings of health and prosperity. Both the *mezuzah*-doorpost scroll and *tefillin*-amulets include this text and other passages on the inscriptions included inside them.

While *mezuzah* literally means "doorpost," today it refers to a small scroll inscribed with passages from the Torah. On the back/outside of the scroll is inscribed *Shaddai*-Provider, one of the names of God and an acronym for the Hebrew, "Guardian of the doors of Israel." The scroll is then mounted on the right doorpost inside a small container which is often very decorative. The *mezuzah*-doorpost scroll both announces to the world that this is a Jewish home and brings blessings on the household. There is some evidence that in ancient times the words, or an abbreviation, were literally carved into the doorposts themselves. It is customary to touch the *mezuzah*-doorpost-scroll with the right hand and kiss that hand upon entering a home (some kiss the hand, then touch the *mezuzah*-doorpost-scroll), similar to how the Torah is kissed in a synagogue.

Tefillin-amulets are usually called "phylacteries" in English, but this is just a Greek word for amulet. They consist of two small square leather boxes containing passages from Torah, and are usually worn on the left arm and forehead during morning weekday prayers. Over the generations they have mainly been used by men. During the time of the Second Temple there is some evidence that *tefillin*-amulets were worn all day. The oldest extant examples of *tefillin*-amulets were found among the Dead Sea Scrolls, which makes them about 2,000 years old.

For kabbalists, wearing *tefillin*-amulets is symbolic of binding oneself to God and uniting one's own being in preparation for addressing God in prayer. There are various traditions and mystical understandings regarding how to wrap the straps of the *tefillin*-amulets around the head and arm. One way of wrapping the strap on the left hand forms the letter *shin*, the letter that represents element of fire and refers to *Shaddai*-Provider, one of the names of God. Wearing *tefillin*-amulets is also considered conducive to meditation.

Although not based on the *Shema*-Listen, the oldest biblical quotations in existence were preserved in the form of the oldest Jewish amulets known. In excavations done in Jerusalem, two strips of silver sheet were discovered that have the Priestly Blessing, one of the most important in Judaism, scratched in them:

> May YHVH bless you and keep you.
> May YHVH shine his face upon you and favor you.
> May YHVH lift up his face toward you and grant you *shalom*-peace. (Numbers 6:24-26)

These silver sheets were then rolled up, a string inserted through the scroll, and worn around the neck as amulets. Found in an ancient Jerusalem tomb, they date to the seventh century BCE (predating the Dead Sea Scrolls by about 400 years) and are inscribed using the paleo-Hebrew script used during the First Temple period.[56]

There are also other amulets that evolved later and continue to be used; they are customary and optional rather than commanded. A *mizrach*-east is a sign, usually ornamental, with the Hebrew word *mizrach* on it. It is placed on the eastern wall of a home to indicate the direction of Jerusalem, which is the direction one faces for prayer.

A *shiviti* is a Jewish mandala; it derives from and is inscribed with "I have set *YHVH*-The Name before me always" (Psalms 16:8), with the *YHVH*-The Name usually in large letters. It is often inscribed with other biblical passages, sometimes in ornate designs, or with kabbalistic permutations of the letters of *YHVH*-The Name. Sometimes printed in kabbalistic books, they were traditionally hung in synagogues, but are now used in homes as well. Kabbalists often use them as a visual focus for meditation on the *YHVH*-The Name.

Another common "good-luck" amulet still in use is a card or scroll with the *tefilat haderech*-traveler's prayer written on it. In Israel today it is often printed on the back of taxi company business cards, perhaps indicating that once you are on the road, your fate is really in God's hands!

In Talmudic and medieval times there was a sense that there were a variety of unseen spirits in the world, many of them evil. Thus, one of the main tasks of the *ba'al shem*-master of The Name was to create amulets for individual protection against particular demons. These always consisted of written words, although there were various magical formulas invoked. Even into the nineteenth century in some parts of the Jewish world amulets were worn by pregnant women to protect their children from Lilith, a demon who they believed tries to strangle newborns. These practices are little used today.

The Holiness of the Body and Sex

> And God created the *adam*-human in his image, in the image of God he created it; male and female he created them. (Genesis 1:27)

> And *YHVH*-The Name, *Elohim*-God, formed the *adam*-human, of dust from the *adamah*-earth. He blew into his nostrils the breath of life, and the *adam*-human became a living soul-being. (Genesis 2:7)

In Genesis it is said that humankind is created in the image of God. For kabbalists this is one of the deepest mysteries of creation. What was the image of the primordial *adam*-human?

One kabbalistic teaching is that *YHVH*-The Name is literally "the image of God" that humans physically emulate, the templates for the creation of humankind. Rabbi Zalman Schachter-Shalomi explains it this way:

So first I will make Earth.
Then I will form the Person out of
My Name, Yud—Heh—Vav—Heh
I will make Yud the head,
Hey the shoulders and arms,
Vav the spine, and
Hey the pelvis and legs.
And then I will blow into its nostrils
and it will become conscious.[57]

Jews believe that *YHVH*-The Name is unpronounceable. One interpretation related by Rabbi Arthur Waskow is that *YHVH* is the sound of vowels only, no consonants, and is the sound of breathing. "The name can be seen as a breath: chest empty, contracted like the *yod*; a breath in, *hay!*; the chest tall and full like a *vav*; and a breath out...*haaaay*. This Breath is the One that when it becomes a word, creates and gives life to all the world."[58] In both Hebrew and English, YHVH-יהוה are neither purely consonants nor vowels; in a sense, they are the liminal letters of the alphabet, conveying our fundamental inability to define a God whose name is "I will be who I will be" (Exodus 3:14).

This breath is the essence of life and one of the ways humans are made in the image of God, for it is the way God gave life to *adam*-human. It was God in both modes, the *Elohim*-God creator and the *YHVH*-The Name unifier that breathed life into the primordial human.

While Adam names all the other creatures in the Garden of Eden, it is God who names Adam. What's in a name? For kabbalists God creates through speech and words; thus words are not accidental labels but descriptive of what is essential. *Gematria*-numerology reveals other connections and hidden meanings. For example, the letters of *adam*-human are *alef* = 1, *dalet* = 4 and *mem* = 40. The alef represents the oneness of God, the dalet represents the four elements from which *adam*-human is made, and the *mem* represents soul level of humankind, for multiplying the four by ten indicates the higher level of creation.

A speculation from the time of the Talmud is that the words "male and female he created them" means that the primordial Adam was androgynous, having the organs of both sexes, attached either back to back or side to side.[59] The *Zohar*-Brightness points out that the Torah is very clear that the term for the original *Adam*-Human is a name for humankind:

> Come and see: The Blessed Holy One does not place His abode in any place where male and female are not found together. Blessings are found only in a place where male and female are found, as it is written: "He blessed them and called their name Adam on the day they were created." (Genesis 5:2)

> It is not written: "He blessed him and called his name Adam." A human being is only called Adam when male and female are as one. (*Zohar* 1:55b)[60]

It is worth following the alchemical aspect of human evolution as depicted in Genesis. The primordial *adam*-human was made of *adamah*-earth and air; breath is what characterizes living beings. Another interpretation is that the name Adam derives from *dam*-blood, which is the element of water. It is also pointed out in the Talmud that the *adamah*-earth also spells *adameh*-I resemble, with only a difference of the vowel points. This resemblance is to God, for there is a phrase in Isaiah (14:14) that reads, "I resemble the Supernal One."[61]

Up to this point the primordial Adam was made up of three of the four basic elements: earth, air, water. Then God decides that, "It is not good for Adam to be alone" (Genesis 2:18). In the Garden of Eden God performs surgery on these Siamese twins, taking the "rib" from Adam (in fact, the "rib" may actually mean "side" in the text) resulting in the split between male and female. Then the man says:

> "She shall be called *ishah*-woman for from *ish*-man she was taken." Therefore a man leaves his father and his mother and clings to his wife, and they become one flesh. (Genesis 2:23-24)

At this point the words change: instead of *adam*-human the terms *ish*-man (spelled *alef-yod-shin*) and *ishah*-woman (spelled *alef-shin-hey*) are used for the first time. Kabbalistically this means that when *adam*-human is separated into man and woman the element of fire is added to their being. By itself, *alef-shin* spells *aish*-fire. In a paradoxical sense, the separation of gender is actually a completion of creation, for now humans are made up of all four alchemical elements and have access to each of the Four Worlds (see the chapter entitled "The Stucture of Reality, the Life of the Soul").

When the yod is inserted into *aish*-fire, the result is *ish*-man and when the hey is appended you get *ishah*-woman. The significance of this becomes clear when man and woman are brought together, for the man brings the fire of the *yod* and the woman brings the fire of the *hey*; together the *yod* and *hey* spell *Yah*, one of the names of God and the first two letters of *YHVH*-The Name.

אש   *esh*-fire

איש   *ish*-man

אשה   *ishah*-woman

יה   *Yah*-God

Furthermore, for the kabbalist the *yod* represents the male principles of seed and energy, while the *hey* represents the female principles of containment and time that brings form; both are necessary to produce the image of God. The *yod* and *hey* also symbolize the *sefirot*-emanations of *Hokhmah*-Wisdom and *Binah*-Understanding, the supernal Father and Mother in the Tree-of-Life who are said to be in an eternal sexual embrace creating the everflowing energy of the cosmos.

In their sexual togetherness man and woman approach the image of God and emulate the embrace of *Hokhmah*-Wisdom and *Binah*-Understanding. In fact, the Bible says that "they become one flesh" in order to reunite; that is the point when we become fully human and adult, leaving our parents' home (Genesis 2:24). That is also when we are most like the image of God that we can become—and for the kabbalist it is no accident that new life springs out of this union, for the creation of new life is humankind's most God-like action.

Another way that kabbalists have looked at the creation story is that the original man and woman were beings of light, at least to our way of understanding. The creation of order out of chaos begins with the creation of light (Genesis 1:3), or energy, to use a more contemporary term. After Adam and Eve eat from the Tree-of-Knowledge of Good and Evil, and just before they are expelled from the Garden of Eden, the Torah says that "YHVH, God, made Adam and his wife coats of skins and clothed them" (Genesis 3:21). What interests the kabbalists is the word *ohr*-skin, where *ohr* is spelled עוֹר *ayin-vav-resh;* it sounds the same as *ohr*-light, spelled אוֹר *alef-vav-resh,* with just the switch of *ayin* for *alef.* In order for humankind to leave the Garden of Eden their light bodies were cloaked by skin to cover and contain their bodies. Prior to leaving the garden they were naked in the sense that only their light-bodies existed, that is, they existed on a level of the soul different from the physical universe in which we are embedded. This enclosure in physical bodies was necessary for the descent to the world of separation, of duality, of relationship, and of mortality.

It is at this point that the woman is renamed *Havva*-Eve, "because she was the mother of all the living" (Genesis 3:20). Yet, it is only after leaving the Garden of Eden that Adam and Eve "know" each other sexually and procreation begins.

Using *gematria*-numerology, kabbalists are able to confirm and expand these meanings of the text. The numerical value of *ahava*-love is thirteen, which is also the numerical value of *echad*-one. When man and woman come together skin-to-skin in love to form one flesh, the numerical value is twenty-six—which is the numerical value of *YHVH*-The Name.

Sex, then, can be both a way to approach God and a way to bring God into the world. Sex is not just for the purpose of procreation, although that is important; sex is to be enjoyed as one of God's gifts. This is, for kabbalists, the reason why sex is so vitalizing—and why it must be handled carefully. Just as we are told in the second commandment to avoid idol worship (Exodus 20:4-5) and in the third commandment not to take God's name in vain (Exodus 20:7), so we must be careful to honor the sacredness of sexuality. We should not make of sex a fetish nor a business—particularly common contemporary forms of idolatry and vanity. The traditional interpretation is that God will be with you if you follow the Torah; otherwise you will become fire. Just as fire is at once both dangerous and the basis of human civilization, many people in our world today have been burned by improper or uncontrolled sexuality. Judaism does not have a monastic tradition and has never encouraged sexual abstinence. In general, marriage has been seen as the proper container for sexual energy, and men and women are seen as incomplete without a mate.

For Jews this means neither repressing sex nor degrading it, for it is a manifestation of the sexual energies of the universe as modeled in the Tree-of-Life. The mystical dimension of Judaism is bound up with a recognition of the sexual dimension of the cosmos. For example, since the seventeenth century, kabbalistic *siddurim*-prayerbooks have included the following mystical preamble to certain prayers:

> For the sake of the unification of the Holy One, blessed is He, and His *Shekhinah*-Presence, in fear and love to unify The Name *yod-hay* with *vav-hey* in perfect unity in the name of Israel.

This is recited in order to arouse the individual's focus; what is being asserted is that sexuality is embodied in *YHVH*-The Name of God, the essence of God and the model for the universe God created. More than that, through proper intent one helps to unite God and God's creation by bringing together the first two letters of *YHVH*-The Name, seen as masculine, with the last two letters, seen as feminine.

The kabbalists of Safed saw *shabbat*-sabbath as a particularly propitious time for sex because it would enhance the holiness of the day, and there is sexual symbolism embedded throughout the symbols of *shabbat*-sabbath and some of the other holidays (see section on "The Week" in the chapter "Kabbalistic Time"). Yet at other times, such as on Yom Kippur—also called the holiest day of the year and the *shabbat*-sabbath of all the *shabbatot*-sabbaths—sex is forbidden, for it would distract us from the main purpose of the holiday, which is one of repentance. On Yom Kippur God acts as Judge and is most distant from us, while on other *shabbatot*-sabbaths God as *Shekhinah*-Presence is most near, for *shabbat*-sabbath is a taste of the messianic world, which will be like the original Garden of Eden.

Kabbalistic Time: The Jewish Calendar and the Holiday Cycle

> To everything there is a season, and a time to every purpose under the heaven. (Ecclesiastes 3:1)

January of the year 2000 CE falls in the middle of the year 5760 according to the Jewish calendar; that is, 5,760 years since the creation of the world described in Genesis 1. As a framework in time that forms and defines the flow of the annual cycle, the Jewish calendar is one of the central pillars of Kabbalah. Many books have been written on the Jewish calendar and the practices embedded therein; all I can do here is give a hint of what is a deep dimension of kabbalistic practice.

As with many other aspects of Kabbalah, the kabbalists start with the calendar used by all Jews, but add layer upon layer of mystical understandings. The calendar is both a map and a plan to the patterns and rhythms we feel and experience, but cannot see, as we sail the ocean of time. It is a map in that it guides us on our way. It is a plan, for as we mark and observe the special holiness of certain times we are actively creating the sacred in time. We are both participants and creators, performing *tikkun*-repair in time.

The calendar used by most of the world to synchronize our civilization's political and economic activities is the Gregorian calendar, named for Pope Gregory XIII, who promulgated it in 1582. Its guiding principle is to synchronize with the orbit of the earth around the sun every 365¼ days, which means it is an accurate representation and predictor of the four seasons of the solar, and agricultural, year. It was only a slight modification of the Roman calendar promulgated by Julius Caesar in 46 BCE. The main Christian modifications to the Roman calendar were the addition of seven-day weeks and changing the year zero to Jesus' birth instead of the founding of Rome. Jews today prefer to call this the civil calendar, since it is the calendar used for public functions in a multicultural world.

The Jewish calendar, sometimes called the Hebrew calendar, has evolved over the 3,000-year history of the Jewish people, and has its roots in even older Babylonian and Canaanite calendars. The best evidence of this is the names of the Hebrew months, which derive from the Babylonian calendar and are named after Babylonian gods or holidays. It continues to evolve even into our era, as the new holidays of Israel Independence Day and Holocaust Memorial Day have been added.

The Jewish calendar is a luni-solar calendar that takes into account both the cycles of the moon and the sun. The annual sun cycle was critical for the agricultural cycle, and many of the holidays are connected to rhythms of the agricultural year. Of equal importance, however, are the moon's cycles of light and dark. Many of the holidays take place on the evening of the full moon, while the appearance of the crescent of the new moon is celebrated as the beginning of a new month, which matches the lunar cycle. In the Bible the appearance of a new moon/month was a holiday on par with other celebrations.

The result is that the months of the Jewish year match the cycles of the moon. The Hebrew months always begin (and end) with the "birth" of a new crescent moon. In fact, the moon is so important that there are two Hebrew words for month, *hodesh* and *yerach*. *Hodesh* means newness and derives from *hadash*-new, referring to the new moon cycle. Of course, the English "month" also derives from "moon," although the astronomical relationship no longer exists. *Yerach* means moon-cycle and is related to *yareyach*-moon. The moon itself is also known as *levanah*, which is related to *lavan*-white, and is a reference to its color.

Over time, two adjustments must be made to keep the fullness of the months in synch with both the daily cycle and the solar year that determines the four *tekufot*-seasons. First, because the cycle of the new moon is approximately 29½ days long, some months vary in length (they vary from year to year). Second, because the moon cycle does not evenly match the annual solar cycle some years have twelve months, others have an additional thirteenth "leap" month. Because the first month of the ancient calendar was in the spring, the additional month is added just before spring. The years themselves can vary in length from 353 to 385 days. This process of intercalation, of inserting additional days and months into the year, results in a fairly complex pattern. The result is a nineteen-year calendrical cycle: every nineteenth year the same date of the Hebrew calendar will fall on the same date of the civil calendar. Out of these nineteen years, seven will be leap years that include an extra month (the month of Adar becomes Adar I and Adar II) which is inserted before the *Pesach*-Passover month of Nisan, so that the spring holiday of *Pesach*-Passover will fall in the correct season. There are books of tables[62] and, more recently, computer programs[63] designed to convert dates between the Jewish and civil calendars. These are useful not only for checking when Jewish Holidays fall on the civil calendar, but also for checking one's Jewish birthday or other dates. One calendar con-

version program available on the Internet can be found at
http://www.uwm.edu/~corre/calendar.html

In the Jewish calendar five cycles of time are embedded in
a dynamic balance: the day, the week, the month, the year,
and groups of years. Note that three of these, the day,
month, year, are cycles of nature that result from the astronomical relationship of the earth's revolution on its axis, the
moon around the earth, and the earth around the sun; these
are also observed in some fashion by non-Jewish cultures.
Knowledge of the other two, the week and groups of years,
are attributed to God's revelation in the Torah.

The Day

"And there was evening and there was morning, a first day."
(Genesis 1:5)

While the cycle of day and night is based on the physical fact
of the earth's spin on its axis, *when* a day is thought to begin
and end varies by culture. While the convention of the civil
calendar, derived from the Roman calendar, is to end and
begin the day at midnight, the Jewish day ends and begins at
sunset, based on the biblical story of creation in Genesis.

But twilight—after the sun sets but before the stars can be
seen—is one of those liminal, "in between" times during
which time itself is neither night nor day. Depending on the
situation, the length of the day can be stretched or com-
pressed. For example, the rules for the beginning and end of

shabbat-sabbath stretch it: *shabbat*-sabbath commences at sunset, but only ends the next night when the sky is dark enough to see three stars. This view of the daily cycle puts us in touch with the cycles of nature.

Indeed, the daily Jewish prayer cycle is linked to these natural cycles. The Jewish custom is to pray three times a day: *Maariv*, or "evening," is the evening prayer; *Sharcharit*, or "dawn," is the morning prayer; *Mincha*, the "offering," is prayed in the afternoon and is tied to the time of day when sacrifices were made in the temple.

Kabbalists believe that evening and morning are particularly auspicious times for prayer because the liminal nature of the light is a reflection in our world of a closeness between our world and other dimensions of reality; it is a time when "the worlds" are closer together, and prayers are more likely to reach heaven.

The Week

> The heaven and the earth were finished, and all their array. On the seventh day God finished the work that He had been doing, and He ceased on the seventh day from all the work that He had done. And God blessed the seventh day and declared it holy, because on it God ceased from all the work of creation that He had done. (Genesis 2:1–4)

> Remember the sabbath day and keep it holy. Six days you shall labor and do all your work, but the seventh day is a sabbath of the Lord your God: you shall not do any work—

you, your son or daughter, your male or female slave, or your cattle, or the stranger who is within your settlements. For in six days the Lord made heaven and earth and sea, and all that is in them, and He rested on the seventh day; therefore the Lord blessed the sabbath day and hallowed it. (Exodus 20:8–11)

The Israelite people shall keep the sabbath, observing the sabbath throughout the ages as a covenant for all time. (Exodus 31:16)[64]

The seven-day cycle of the week that we take for granted today is not a cycle deriving from the natural world. Calendars from cultures around the world gather days of various numbers into groups of time less than a month. The week of the civil calendar derives from the seven day cycle of the Jewish *shabbat*-sabbath, which was adopted by early Christians. The *shabbat*-sabbath forms the week into a fundamental rhythm of human time between work and rest, a rhythm that overlays the monthly and yearly cycles of moon and sun.

For kabbalists, as for Jews in general, *shabbat*-sabbath is a divine decree. One seventh of our time on earth is to be set aside as holy, for rest. The Jewish week revolves around *shabbat*-sabbath, which is the name of the seventh day of the week (the Hebrew word *shavua*-week is derived from *sheva*-seven); the other days are called by their number: first day, second day, etc. The special rules and rituals that surround the *shabbat*-sabbath are multiple and reinforcing, and provide a regular entryway into sacred time and sacred space. Because *shabbat*-sabbath is not a function of a cycle of nature, our participation in the rituals of *shabbat*-sabbath are what create it; the Hebrew word *la'asot*, often translated as "to observe" also means "to make" *shabbat*-sabbath.

Kabbalistic views and practices concerning the *shabbat*-sabbath are perhaps some of the most pervasive elements of Kabbalah in general Jewish practice. The sixteenth century kabbalists of Safed developed many of the rituals and liturgy now considered traditional for *shabbat*-sabbath. For example, one of the most well-known *shabbat*-sabbath evening hymns, "*Lekhah Dodi*-Come My Beloved," was composed by Rabbi Shlomo Alkabetz, and sanctioned by Rabbi Isaac Luria. The first two lines, which are the refrain of this long and lovely poem, are:

> Come, my beloved, to meet the bride
> The *shabbat*-sabbath presence, let us welcome!

The "beloved" is whoever you are with, sharing this *shabbat*-sabbath, and alludes to passages in the Song of Songs. The "bride" is the *shabbat*-sabbath, for the Jewish people are considered "wedded" to *shabbat*-sabbath. At the same time, "beloved" is God in His male aspect; the "bride" is Shekhinah, God in Her female aspect. Thus, making *shabbat*-sabbath unites the Jews in the observance of *shabbat*-sabbath, unites the Jewish people with *shabbat*-sabbath, and reenacts the *heiros-gamos* of the divine wedding reuniting the male and female aspects of God. *Shabbat*-sabbath eve is also considered a particularly propitious time for husbands and wives to enjoy sex, both for its pleasure and the union of the male and female energies of the cosmos.

All this amounts to a cosmic *tikkun*-repair on many levels, bringing us closer to God and Godliness. *Shabbat*-sabbath is known as a "taste of the world to come," that is, of the messianic era of wholeness when all separation and alienation will disappear. For kabbalists, life is lived from *shabbat*-sabbath to *shabbat*-sabbath.

The Month

> And on your joyous occasions—your fixed festivals and new moon days—you shall sound the trumpets over your burnt offerings and your sacrifices of well-being. (Numbers 10:10)
>
> Blow the horn on the new moon, on the full moon for our feast day (Psalms 81:4)[65]

The importance of the moon cycle for Jewish holidays reflects the agricultural and rural culture of the people, for the cycle of the moon strongly influences the ease with which public evening activity can take place. *Rosh Hodesh*-New Moon celebrates the ending of the waning period of the moon-cycle and the beginning of the waxing period, as we begin to leave the darkest part of the month. The *shabbat*-sabbath before a new moon is called "the *shabbat*-sabbath of blessing," for prayers are said asking for a good month. The is a special blessing said upon sighting the new moon, the *kiddush levanah*. The arrival of *Rosh Hodesh*-New Moon is a celebration of rebirth of the moon, which symbolizes the waning and waxing in our own lives; each new moon reminds us that light follows darkness, that as difficult as things may get there is always a time for renewed optimism. In life there are times for inwardness and withdrawal, which are often necessary preludes to the display of new beginnings, just as the darkness of the womb is the start of new life.

In the last twenty-five years *Rosh Hodesh*-New Moon has been adopted by Jewish women, especially in North America, and has evolved into a monthly women's observance and festival. The basis for this adoption is a Talmudic story that says that at Mount Sinai women refused to give their gold for the construction of the Golden Calf, and God rewarded them by having them observe the New Moons more than men. There is also a recognition of the connection to women's monthly cycle, after which they renew themselves through a ritual bath and are once again fertile. Over the centuries women were encouraged to not work on that day, particularly spinning, weaving and sewing, and laundry. There is an ancient custom to have a festive meal on *Rosh Hodesh*-New Moon, and this has been incorporated into contemporary *Rosh Hodesh*-New Moon observances.[66]

In the Zohar-Brightness, the moon is seen as a feminine symbol of the *Shekhinah*-Presence, who receives illumination from the sun, symbol of male energy of the Blessed Holy One.[67] The Jewish People are seen as protected by the "wings of the *Shekhinah*-Presence," who is with them in their exile. Like the *Shekhinah*-Presence, the Jewish People are seen as the feminine lover of the Blessed Holy One as expressed in the passionate love poetry of the Song of Songs. The waxing and waning of the moon's cycle is like the variations in our own connection with God.

When the Temple stood, the new moon was determined by visual sighting, and was celebrated by an additional sacrifice and the sounding of trumpets. Later on the Rabbis became more astronomically sophisticated and developed an accurate mathematical procedure for determining the new moons. The kabbalists of sixteenth century Safed developed a series of rituals for the day before *Rosh Hodesh*-New Moon, which they called a "miniature Yom Kippur." These included fasting, giving of charity and special prayers. For these kabbalists, the moon embodied the kabbalistic notion of the dynamic balance between the cosmic force of expansiveness, associated with *Hesed*-Unbounded Love and the right side of the Tree-of-Life versus the cosmic force of contraction, associated with *Gevurah*-Strength and the left side of the Tree-of-Life. As the moon wanes and darkness increases, the forces of *Gevurah*-Strength are ascendant. At the darkest point of the moon cycle, the point where the sun, earth, and moon are "gathered" together in cosmological alignment, the moon is between the earth and the sun.[68] At this point the earth is, at least figuratively, most separate from sun (when a perfect alignment occurs the result is an eclipse). But just at this point of total darkness the moon becomes renewed and begins to wax; for kabbalists, this represents the ascendance of *Hesed*-Unbounded Love over *Gevurah*-Strength. This inflection point, this transition to a new month, was seen as a propitious time for internal *t'shuvah*-turning/repentance in preparation for a time of renewal.

The Year

> God formed twelve constellations in the universe, twelve
> months in the year. (*Sefer Yetzirah*-Book of Formation 5:3)

The Jewish year is a spiral of spirals; the year is the spiral of the earth around the sun, the months the spiral of the moon around the earth. As can be seen in Table 4: Associations of the Months of the Jewish Calendar, the Jewish year consists of twelve months; occasionally a thirteenth month is added, known as Adar II, in order to keep the celebration of the holidays in their proper seasons. The associations of the months with the twelve tribes and the twelve signs of the zodiac is ancient. Indeed, the zodiac and four seasons are common decorative motifs in synagogues from the oldest archeological finds, which date from the Roman period, to the present.

Taken together, the holidays mark our passage through the cycle of the year. The most important holidays take place at

TABLE 4: ASSOCIATIONS OF THE MONTHS OF THE JEWISH CALENDAR

JEWISH MONTH	SECULAR MONTH	SIGN	HOLIDAYS
NISSAN	March–Apr.	Aries	Pesach*
IYAR	Apr.–May	Taurus	Lag Ba-Omer*
SIVAN	May–June	Gemini	Shavuot
TAMUZ	June–July	Cancer	
AV	July–Aug.	Leo	Tisha B'Av, Tu B'Av*
ELUL	Aug.–Sept.	Virgo	
TISHREI	Sept.–Oct.	Libra	Rosh Hashanah Yom Kippur Sukkot*, Shemini Atzeret, Simchat Torah
CHESHVAN	Oct.–Nov.	Scorpio	
KISLEV	Nov.–Dec.	Sagittarius	Hanukkah
TEVET	Dec.–Jan.	Capricorn	Hanukkah
SHEVAT	Jan.–Feb.	Aquarius	Tu Bi-Shevat*
ADAR (OR ADAR I & II)**	Feb.–Mar.	Pisces	Purim*

*Falls on or near the full moon
**A leap year adds another month, resulting in Adar I and Adar II

the inflection points of the year, the spring and fall equinoxes. In the spring *Pesach*-Passover is celebrated as the winter is past and the fullness of the earth begins to show. In the fall, *Rosh Hashanah*-New Year, *Yom Kippur*-Atonement Day and *Sukkot*-Booths (also known as "the festival of Gathering" the harvest) form a three-week period known as "the Holidays."

While all the new moons are celebrated, it is perhaps no accident that half of the months have a holiday that falls on or near the full moon: *Sukkot*-Booths, *Tu Bishvat*-15 of Shvat, *Purim*-Lots, *Pesach*-Passover, *Lag Ba'omer*-33 of the Omer, *Tu B'av*-15 of Av. Some modern kabbalists have noted that the fifteenth of the month, the typical date for a full moon is traditionally spelled by the letters *tet* and *vav*, which have the numerical values of nine and six, adding to fifteen, forming an acronym pronounced *Tu* (hence the name of some of the holidays—*Tu Bishvat* literally means "the fifteenth of the month of Shvat"); the reason for this is the traditional aversion to using the letters for ten and five, *yod* and *hey*, which together form the word "*Yah*," one of the names of God. Thus, the fullness of the moon also represents a fullness of our relation with God at a time in the moon cycle when the earth is aligned between the sun and moon, gathering the rays of both heavenly lights. The <u>Zohar</u>-Brightness observes that at this time "these beloved crowns stand opposite each other,"[69] the male and female aspects of God in both fullness and balance.

On the other hand it is clear that some holidays should not be on the full moon. *Rosh Hashanah*-Head of the Year falls on a new moon, and *Hanukah*-Dedication is the festival of light which takes place during the new moon of the winter solstice, the darkest time of the year.

For kabbalists there are deep and multiple significances to each and every one of the holidays that encompass the agricultural, historical, and mystical dimensions. For example, the Torah commands that after *Pesach*-Passover "you shall count off seven weeks. They must be complete: you must count until the day after the seventh week—fifty days" (Leviticus 23:15–16). The festival of the fiftieth day is *Shavuot*-Weeks, because it is a week of weeks. In the Bible this is an agricultural harvest festival. By the time of the Talmud it had evolved to include the historical dimension: just as *Pesach*-Passover celebrated leaving Egypt, *Shavuot*-Weeks celebrates the revelation of the Torah on Mount Sinai.

The revelation of the Torah is certainly the greatest mystical event of the Bible, and it is no wonder that the kabbalists looked for multiple dimensions of meaning. The word used for "count" in relation to the fifty days between *Pesach*-Passover and *Shavuot*-Weeks is *sefirah*, so the kabbalists related the *sefirah*-counting of days to the *sefirot*-emanations of the Tree-of-Life. The kabbalists came to see that each of the seven weeks is characterized by the energy of one of the lower seven *sefirot*-emanations of the Tree-of-Life, and each day of each week is also characterized by one of the lower seven *sefirot*-emanations. Thus, each day is a unique combination of two different divine energies, that of the day and that of the week. Thus, the "counting" commanded by the Torah becomes a mystical focus for attention to the unique energy of the day defined by the *sefirot*-emanations of that day. By counting and attuning oneself, the kabbalist recapitulates the wandering of the Israelites in the desert on their way to Mount Sinai, becoming spiritually prepared for celebrating and reliving the revelation of the Torah at Mount Sinai.

Groups of Years: Sabbatical, Jubilee, and Cosmic Cycles

> The seventh year, the year of release, is at hand.
> (Deuteronomy 15:9)

The Bible also discusses cycles of years. Every seven years was a sabbatical year, during which no agricultural work could be done: "it shall be a *shabbat*-sabbath of solemn rest for the land" (Leviticus 25:4). People were to live off what was saved from prior years or what grew without human intervention. The seventh year was also known as the *shmittah*-release, for all debts were canceled at that time.

After seven times seven sabbaticals, the fiftieth year was to be a *yovel*-jubilee; this numbering echoes the fifty days between *Pesach*-Passover and *Shavuot*-Weeks. During the jubilee you are to "proclaim liberty throughout the land to all its inhabitants" (Leviticus 25:10). This meant that each family got back the equal portion of the land given their forebear and indentured servants were released. Like a sabbatical, no agricultural work was done.

The kabbalists looked at these patterns of years described in the Torah and saw something deeper. They viewed these as allusions to cosmic eons, which they called *shemittot*; each cosmic day is equated to 1,000 years and each cosmic week is under the influence of one of the lower seven *sefirot*-emanations; after 6,000 years the sabbath-like *shemittah*-eon takes place and the world falls into chaos; after the seventh millennium a new cycle begins under the influence of the following *sefirah*-emanation. But don't start worrying yet; there is some difference of opinion about how long a "year" is in our terms, and whether there is a radical or gradual end to each period.

Many kabbalistic writings assert that our era is only one of a series of eons of creation. While there is no consistency among these speculations, there is a sense that other universes existed and died out before ours came into being. Indeed, there is some thought that the existence of evil in our world is a remnant of these older worlds. They couldn't survive because they were out of balance, but echoes of their negative energy continue to disrupt our world.

Astrology

> Now let me tell you hidden truths. You already know that there are twelve constellations from which the twelve months of the year get their power. Each constellation for the needs of its month. And in this way the constellations and the months draw their sustenance and their food from the name YHVH, may He be Blessed. Know that the twelve constellations which are in the heavens and sustain the lower creatures receive their power from the twelve seals [permutations] of the great name YHVH, may He be Blessed. They unite and join with them, and these twelve seals you will find on four banners, thus you find four seasons in a year. In this format you will find in Israel twelve tribes and four banners in the manner of the twelve seals of the name and their four banners. (Rabbi Joseph Gikatilla, _Sha'are Orah_-Gates of Light)[70]

The astrological aspect of Judaism is so deeply rooted that most Jews today invoke the importance of astrology without even realizing it. Whenever a Jew says _mazal tov_, which is used in the sense of "congratulations," in fact one is literally saying "good constellation," meaning that this event was marked by a good alignment in the heavens. _Mazal_ means "luck," but it is derived from its meaning as "constellation." One of the songs sung at the completion of a Jewish wedding goes: _Mazal tov ve-siman tov_-a good constellation and a good sign, which is to say, may this wedding be marked by good fortune in the heavens!

In fact, there is a very large literature of kabbalistic astrology, which may seem strange, given the biblical injunction against soothsayers. The way the Rabbis resolved this is to say that character analyses through astrology are allowed, but predictions are forbidden. In general, it is believed that the planets and constellations are channels through which spiritual forces come down to the physical plane, but that by virtue of the Jews' receiving the Torah, they are lifted above the influence of the stars. The _Zohar_-Brightness states,

> Before the Torah was given to Israel all the creatures in the world depended on the planets, even in matters of children, livelihood, and sustenance. But after the Torah was given to Israel [the Holy One, blessed be He] excluded them from planetary control....Hence, whoever studies Torah releases himself from planetary control, as long as he studies it in order to carry out its commandments. If this is not the case, it is as if he does not study it at all, and he remains under the control of the stars and the planets.[71]

Thus, the more a person follows Torah and pursues a spiritual practice, especially through prayer, the more they can avoid fate and the natural course of events, because God will respond to their prayer.

One of the major topics of _Sefer Yetzirah_-Book of Formation is astrology, and the book implies many connections between the structure of the _sefirot_-emanations, the Hebrew alphabet, and the astrological aspects of the universe. Many kabbalistic commentaries expanded upon these elements of _Sefer Yetzirah_-Book of Formation. A number of these commentaries relate the twelve astrological signs, the twelve months, the twelve tribes, the twelve astrological houses, and the twelve permutations of *YHVH*-The Name. As stated by Rabbi Joseph Gikatilla in the quote above from _Sha'are Orah_-Gates of Light, the most important association for the kabbalist is this last one, for it is the permutation of *YHVH*-The Name that really sets the energy of the month.

It is important to note that while the associations are similar to those of Western astrology (all traditions of Western astrology evolved out of ancient Babylonia), the Hebrew calendar is lunar oriented, while contemporary Western astrology is strictly solar, reflecting its Roman roots. Thus, while there is an overlap of the solar and lunar signs, every year this overlap between the Hebrew and Gregorian calendars is different (throughout the nineteen-year cycle of the Hebrew calendar). Thus, a person's birthday can be under one sign for Western astrology and a different sign according to the Hebrew calendar. It is thought that a person with a Jewish soul would get a more accurate reading by using their birth sign according to the Jewish calendar. For those interested in checking their birthday and birth sign, remember that the Hebrew day begins at sunset rather than midnight.

Some Problems with Traditional Kabbalah

> Moses stood up in the gate of the camp and said, "Whoever is for the Lord, come here!" And all the Levites rallied to him. He said to them, "Thus says the Lord, the God of Israel: Each of you put sword on thigh, go back and forth from gate to gate throughout the camp, and slay brother, neighbor and kin." The Levites did as Moses had bidden; and some three thousand of the people fell that day. (Exodus 32:26–28)[72]

As we have discussed, Kabbalah can claim an ancient lineage. The development of the Kabbalah has been an intrinsic, even sustaining element, in Judaism. Part of the vibrancy of the Jewish civilization is its resiliency in the face of new developments and changes, both within the Jewish community and between the Jews and non-Jews among whom the Jews have lived in many places over the years. Many strata of ideas and practices have become popular, while others have diminished. Thus, Jewish tradition is rich, both in resources that can be recovered and in those that shouldn't.

We must confront the fact that at the same time many of us search through traditional Jewish sources for elements of wisdom to enrich our practice today and connect with the braid of tradition, there are also elements of the tradition that we will find problematic. Whether one is unreligious or devoutly orthodox in practice, there is always a choice made from the tradition of what is appropriate to practice today. A simple example in the Orthodox world concerns which foods are allowed to be eaten during *Pesach*-Passover. While all agree that eating any type of wheat product other than matzoh is forbidden, the *Mizrahi*-Oriental tradition allows the consumption of rice and beans while the *Ashkenazi*-European tradition forbids those items. My point is that either view is a choice, a matter of interpretation and implementation in particular circumstances.

Therefore, I want to briefly address some of the difficult aspects of traditional Kabbalah that are usually glossed over. Just as the Kabbalah itself recognizes an evil element to our world, there seem to be dysfunctional elements within the Kabbalah itself. These largely have to do with relations between "us" and "other": other individuals, other groups of people, other genders, other species. Rather than encouraging our recognition of the unity of God's creation, they persist in making more distinctions. Living in a global civilization, we can recognize many of these "traditional" attitudes as divisive and chauvinistic. Changing these, or leaving them behind, is also part of the evolution of the Jewish people and the kabbalistic tradition, weaving new strands into the braid of tradition.

Messianism

The mystical perspective has often lead to messianism. The view that through mystical practice one could either compel God to action or help God "heal" the world has always included the restoration of Jewish sovereignty in the Land of Israel and the resumption of the sacrifices commanded by the Torah in a rebuilt Third Temple. Throughout the 2,000 years of the Jewish diaspora (since the destruction of the Second Temple in seventy CE by the Romans) it was thought that if these things came to pass, the arrival of the Messiah would be at hand. Living in precarious circumstances, Jews understandably desired this arrival and often identified a charismatic leader as the Messiah.

During the Roman era, the second Jewish Revolt of 132–135 CE was led by Bar Kochba, who was hailed as the Messiah, and was even endorsed by Rabbi Akiva, the preeminent spiritual leader of the period. Both were killed by the Romans, along with thousands of others. In more recent times, besides the messianic activity of Shabbetai Zevi, we also know that Abraham Abulafia thought he might be the Messiah, and some of the followers of Isaac Luria believed he was the Messiah. In our own day, many Habad Hasidim considered the last Lubavitcher Rebbe to be the Messiah.

For many religious and mystical Jews, Israeli independence, particularly the control of the whole Land of Israel after the 1967 Six Day War, is seen as the "footsteps of the Messiah," a portent that messianic times are afoot. This attitude manifests itself in Israeli political and social life today, where many Jewish settlers in the West Bank (also known by the biblical place names of *Yehudah*-Judah and *Shomron*-Samaria) have a mystical view of their attachment to the land, promised by God to the Jewish People in the bible. The combination of mysticism with nationalistic messianism can lead to perfect faith in one's own perspective without regard for other people and nations. Today groups in Jerusalem study the ancient rituals in preparation for the rebuilding of the Temple, which they believe is imminent. Indeed, some activists tied to these groups have conspired, so far unsuccessfully, to blow up the Islamic mosques that have stood on the Temple mount—the site of the Second Temple—for the last 1,300 years, so that the Third Temple could be built. Messianic attitudes have also played a key role in violence by Jewish messianists, including the assassination of Israeli Prime Minister Yitzhak Rabin by Yigal Amir, and the murder of dozens of Arabs praying at Abraham's Tomb in Hebron by

Baruch Goldstein. Both of these gunmen were convinced that their actions were commanded by God.

Us Versus Them

These contemporary phenomena draw on certain tendencies within traditional Kabbalah that not only identifies the Jews as the chosen people, but asserts that this chosenness means that Jews not only have a special path to God, but the only true path to God. The important contemporary kabbalist Rabbi Aryeh Kaplan, for example, asserts in a long discussion of the mystical significance of circumcision that "a person cannot have a true spiritual experience unless he can latch on to *Yesod* in a circumcised state."[73] This is traditionally understood to exclude all women and non-Jewish men (even though some non-Jewish men are circumcised).

This tradition of superiority, while an understandable perspective for a persecuted minority trying to preserve its integrity, is no longer appropriate in a multicultural world society where all peoples must recognize that they may have *a* truth, but not *the* exclusive truth. There are more tolerant views in the Jewish religious and mystical tradition, and these must also be given voice today. Notions of superiority in our world today are a dangerous form of idolatry.

Sexuality and Gender

It is well known that Kabbalah was primarily a male spiritual tradition. Despite a large amount of feminine and genderful imagery, it is clear that the gender images are strongly patriarchal. Part of its perspective was the association of women with evil. Both women and evil were associated with the left side of the Tree-of-Life, particularly the *sefirah*-emanation of *Gevurah*-Power, and a surplus of this energy is what gives rise to the evil realm referred to in the <u>Zohar</u>-Brightness as the *sitra ahra*-other side. The semen produced during masturbation or nocturnal emissions was seen as providing Lilith, the female consort of the Samael, the equivalent of Satan in the <u>Zohar</u>-Brightness, with seed to give birth to demons.[74]

These medieval perspectives are not only unappealing, they are repulsive to most contemporary sensibilities. This is part of what is being left behind as contemporary Jewish kabbalists emphasize more affirmative views of our body, sexuality, gender, and a more positive view of the relationship of Jews to non-Jews. Kabbalah, like other aspects of Jewish life, continues to evolve today as a living tradition, infused by the creative energies of women and men who join the wisdom of the past with the promise of life today. This is how the braid of tradition—the Kabbalah—lives.

Notes

1. Daniel C. Matt, *The Essential Kabbalah: The Heart of Jewish Mysticism* (San Francisco: Harper San Francisco, 1995), p. 160.

2. Ibid., p. 83.

3. Yitzhak Buxbaum, *Jewish Spiritual Practices* (Northvale, New Jersey: Jason Aronson, Inc., 1990), p. 4.

4. Gershom Scholem, *Major Trends in Jewish Mysticism* (New York: Schocken Books, 1961, Third Revised Edition), p. 37.

5. Chava Weissler, "Woman as High Priest: A Kabbalistic Prayer in Yiddish for Lighting Sabbath Candles," in *Essential Papers on Kabbalah*, ed. Lawrence Fine (New York: New York University Press, 1995), pp. 525-546, 529.

6. Zalman Schachter-Shalomi, *Paradigm Shift* (Northvale, New Jersey: Jason Aronson Inc., 1993b), pp. 292.

7. Moshe Idel, *Kabbalah: New Perspectives* (New Haven: Yale University Press, 1988a), pp. xi-xiii.

8. Gershom Scholem, *Kabbalah* (New York: Meridian, 1978), p. 4.

9. Zalman Schachter-Shalomi, *Paradigm Shift* , pp. 266-268; David A. Cooper, *God Is a Verb: Kabbalah and the Practice of Mystical Judaism* (New York: Riverhead Books, 1997), p. 64.

10. Louis Jacobs, *Jewish Mystical Testimonies* (New York: Schocken Books, 1977), p. 38.

11. Ibid., p. 32.

12. Ibid., p. 29.

13. Aryeh Kaplan, *Sefer Yetzirah: The Book of Creation* (York Beach, Maine: Samuel Weiser, 1990), pp. 5, 22.

14. Isaiah Tishby, ed. *The Wisdom of the Zohar: An Anthology of Texts*, III vols. (Washington: The Littman Library of Jewish Civilization, 1994), p. 312.

15. Aryeh Kaplan, *Sefer Yetzirah*, pp. 129-130.

16. Ibid., pp. 126-128.

17. Ben Zion Bokser, *The Jewish Mystical Tradition* (Northvale, New Jersey: Jason Aronson Inc., 1993), p. 11.

18. Ibid., pp. 85-86.

19. Zalman Schachter-Shalomi, *Gate to the Heart: An Evolving Process* (Philadelphia: ALEPH: Alliance for Jewish Renewal, 1993a), p. 56.

20. Yonassan Gershom, *49 Gates of Light: Kabbalistic Meditations for Counting the Omer* (Sandstone, MN: Gershom Enterprises, 1987), p. 6.

21. Zalman Schachter-Shalomi, *Gate to the Heart*, 50-51.

22. Ibid., p. 56.

23. Ibid.

24. Ibid.; Aryeh Kaplan, *Innerspace: Introduction to Kabbalah, Meditation and Prophecy* (Jerusalem: Moznaim Publishing Corporation, 1991), p. 45.

25. Aryeh Kaplan, *Meditation and Kabbalah* (York Beach, Maine: Samuel Weiser, Inc., 1985), p. 126

26. Ibid.

27. Yonassan Gershom, *49 Gates of Light: Kabbalistic Meditations for Counting the Omer*, p. 75

28. Aryeh Kaplan, *Sefer Yetzirah*, p. 184.

29. Ibid. pp. 44-45, 57; Aryeh Kaplan, *The Bahir* (Northvale, New Jersey: Jason Aronson Inc., 1995), p. 107.

30. Aryeh Kaplan, *Sefer Yetzirah*, pp. 46, 164-165.

31. Aryeh Kaplan, *Innerspace*, p. 45.

32. Aryeh Kaplan, *Sefer Yetzirah*, p. 6; English Translation from *Tanakh: A New Translation of The Holy Scriptures According to the Traditional Hebrew Text* (Philadelphia: The Jewish Publication Society, 1985), pp. 3-4.

33. Gershom Scholem, *Kabbalah*, p. 6.

34. Moshe Idel, *The Mystical Experience in Abraham Abulafia*, trans. Jonathan Chipman (Albany: State University of New York Press, 1988b), pp. 13-17.

35. Aryeh Kaplan, *Meditation and Kabbalah*, p. 64.

36. Gershom Scholem, *Kabbalah*, p. 420.

37. Lawrence Kushner, *Invisible Lines of Connection: Sacred Stories of the Ordinary* (Woodstock, Vermont: Jewish Lights, 1996).

38. Rodger Kamenetz, *The Jew In the Lotus* (San Francisco: HarperSanFrancisco, 1994), pp. 226-234.

39. Aryeh Kaplan, *Meditation and Kabbalah*, p. 32.

40. Gershom Scholem, *Kabbalah*, p. 197.

41. Ibid., pp. 196-203.

42. Daniel Chanan Matt, ed. *Zohar: The Book of Enlightenment* (New York: Paulist Press, 1983), p. 45.

43. Bahya ben Asher in Daniel C. Matt, *The Essential Kabbalah*, p. 146.

44. Isaiah Tishby, ed. *The Wisdom of the Zohar*, p. 312.

45. *Tanakh*

46. Marcia Falk, *The Book of Blessings* (San Francisco: HarperSanFrancisco, 1996), p. 170.

47. Lynn Gottlieb, *She Who Dwells Within* (San Francisco: HarperSanFrancisco, 1995), p. 33.

48. Matityahu Glazerson, *Torah, Light and Healing* (Northvale, New Jersey: Jason Aronson Inc., 1996), pp. 29-30.

49. Gershom Scholem, *Kabbalah*, p. 338.

50. Ibid., p. 172.

51. Daniel C. Matt, *The Essential Kabbalah*, p. 48.

52. I have gathered these associations from many places. See especially Zalman Schachter-Shalomi, *Gate to the Heart*, p. 57 and Simcha Paull Raphael, *Jewish Views of the Afterlife* (Northvale, New Jersey: Jason Aronson, Inc., 1994), pp. 366-367.

53. Isaiah Tishby, ed. *The Wisdom of the Zohar*, pp. 733-735.

54. Aryeh Kaplan, *Sefer Yetzirah*, pp. xxi, 348.

55. Joshua Trachtenberg, *Jewish Magic and Superstition: A Study in Folk Religion* (New York: Atheneum, 1977 (1939)), p. 236.

56. Hershel Shanks, *Jerusalem: An Archaeological Biography* (New York: Random House, 1995), p. 118.

57. Zalman Schachter-Shalomi, *Paradigm Shift*, p. 302.

58. Arthur I. Waskow, *Seasons of Our Joy: A Handbook of Jewish Festivals* (New York: Bantam Books, 1982), p. 55.

59. Daniel Chanan Matt, ed. *Zohar*, p. 217.

60. Ibid., p. 56.

61. Matityahu Glazerson, *Torah, Light and Healing* (Northvale, New Jersey: Jason Aronson Inc., 1996), p. 158.

62. Arthur Spier, *The Comprehensive Hebrew Calendar*, Third, Revised Edition ed. (Nanuet, NY: Feldheim Publishers, 1986).

63. Zmanim: The Hebrew Calendar (Chicago: Davka Software).

64. Translations from *Tanakh*.

65. Ibid.

66. Susan Berrin, ed. *Celebrating the New Moon: A Rosh Chodesh Anthology* (Northvale, New Jersey: Jason Aronson Inc., 1996), pp. 6-7.

67. Isaiah Tishby, ed. *The Wisdom of the Zohar*, p. 404.

68. Susan Berrin, ed. *Celebrating the New Moon*, p. 134.

69. Isaiah Tishby, ed. *The Wisdom of the Zohar*, p. 404.

70. Translation adapted from Joseph Gikatilla, *Sha'are Orah: Gates of Light*, trans. Avi Weinstein (San Francisco: Harper Collis, 1994), pp. 232-233.

71. Isaiah Tishby, ed. *The Wisdom of the Zohar*, p. 1432.

72. Translation from *Tanakh*.

73. Aryeh Kaplan, *Innerspace*, p. 175.

74. Gershom Scholem, *Kabbalah*, pp. 124-125, 322.

Go and Learn

Kabbalistic Texts

Bokser, Ben Zion, ed. *The Jewish Mystical Tradition*. Jason Aronson.

Chronological anthology of Jewish mystical writings.

Jacobs, Louis, ed. *Jewish Mystical Testimonies*. Schocken Books.

Documents of Jewish Mystical experience from the Bible to the twentieth century.

Kaplan, Aryeh, trans. *The Bahir*. Jason Aronson.

Translation and commentary of a classic kabbalistic text that delineates the ten *sefirot*, their relation to anthropomorphism, and the reason for the commandments.

Kaplan, Aryeh, trans. *Meditation and Kabbalah*. Jason Aronson.

A rich collection of classical texts, exploring the meditative techniques of medieval kabbalists.

Kaplan, Aryeh, trans. *Sefer Yetzirah: The Book of Creation*. Jason Aronson.

Translation and commentary of one of the oldest kabbalistic texts, including meditations, angelic connections, and astrological aspects.

Matt, Daniel, ed. *The Essential Kabbalah: The Heart of Jewish Mysticism*. Harper Collins.

An anthology of kabbalistic writings, including an interpretive essay.

Matt, Daniel, ed. *Zohar—The Book of Enlightenment*. Paulist Press.

Excerpts from the most important text of the Kabbalah, along with an interpretive essay discussing the Tree-of-Life.

History of Kabbalah

Scholem, Gershom. *Kabbalah*. Meridian.

A collection of Scholem's articles for the *Encyclopaedia Judaica*. The most comprehensive single volume on the Kabbalah, covering its historical development and major concepts and personalities.

Scholem, Gershom. *Major Trends in Jewish Mysticism*. Schocken.

The first, classic work in the scholarly field of Kabbalah.

Contemporary Jewish Mysticism, Spirituality, and Kabbalah

Cooper, David A. *God Is a Verb*. Riverhead Books.

An extensive, readable exposition of contemporary Kabbalah, including meditative exercises.

Falk, Marcia. *The Book of Blessings*. Harper San Francisco.

A prayer book in Hebrew and English, rewritten with an egalitarian, feminist perspective.

Fisdel, Steven. *The Practice of Kabbalah: Meditation in Judaism*. Jason Aronson.

A step-by-step guide into the realm of kabbalistic meditation, including contemporary versions of classical meditative techniques such as focusing on the Hebrew alphabet, the *sefirot*, and the names of God.

Gershom, Yonassan. *49 Gates of Light: Kabbalistic Meditations for Counting the Omer*. Gershom Enterprises.

An interesting spiral-bound guide to incorporating kabbalistic practice into your life during the period between the holidays of *Pesach*-Passover and *Shavuot*-Weeks.

Gottlieb, Lynn. *She Who Dwells Within*. Harper San Francisco. Describes a re-awakening of the feminine and feminist dimension within Judaism.

Hoffman, Edward, ed. *Opening the Inner Gates*. Shambhala.

A collection of essays connecting Kabbalah and modern psychology.

Kamenetz, Roger. *The Jew in the Lotus*. Harper San Francisco.

The story of a meeting between a group of Rabbis and the Dalai Lama, including discussions of the similarities and differences between Judaism and Tibetan Buddhism.

Kushner, Lawrence. *Honey from the Rock*. Jewish Lights.

A modern classic introducing Kabbalah.

Raphael, Simcha Paull. *Jewish Views of the Afterlife*. Jason Aronson.

A thorough exploration of Jewish thought and speculation on the afterlife, including kabbalistic views of the four worlds and the levels of the soul, and the connection to contemporary psychological models.

Schachter-Shalomi, Zalman. *Gate to the Heart: An Evolving Process*. Aleph: Alliance for Jewish Renewal.

Discussion and instructions concerning kabbalistic meditation and prayer practice, including illustrations.

Schachter-Shalomi, Zalman. *Paradigm Shift*. Jason Aronson.

Offers a unique blend of Jewish mystical ideas as they encounter the forces and sensibilities of today, as the author develops his ideas concerning Jewish Renewal.

Waskow, Arthur. *Seasons of Our Joy*. Bantam Books.

A contemporary guide to the Jewish holidays.

Tapes
Cooper, Rabbi David A. *The Mystical Kabbalah*.

An excellent 5-cassette study guide that includes stories, meditations and explanations of Kabbalah.

Zeller, Rabbi David. *The Tree of Life*.

This is an excellent six-cassette study guide that includes stories, prayers, meditations, and sacred practice of Kabbalah.

Cards
Feldman, Ron. *Kabbalah Cards*.

A seventy-eight-card deck (the same as a Tarot deck) utilizing the symbolism of the Jewish Kabbalah: the Hebrew letters, the *sefirot*-emanations, the four worlds, and the Tree-of-Life.

BOOKS BY THE CROSSING PRESS

Caretaking a New Soul: Writings on Parenting from Thich Nhat Hanh to Z. Budapest

Edited by Anne Carson

This book is a collection of writings on parenting that brings together ideas, suggestions, practices, and advice from parents of diverse beliefs. Suggestions for ceremonies and rituals to mark special times are included.

$14.95 • Paper • ISBN 0-58091-018-1

Circumcision Exposed: Rethinking a Medical and Cultural Tradition

By Billy Ray Boyd

Infant male circumcision is the most commonly performed surgery in the U.S., about 3,000 every day. This book will have a profound impact on a ritual more than 2,000 years old and will change outmoded methods of thinking.—from the Foreword by Paul M. Fleiss, M.D.

$14.95 • Paper • ISBN 0-89594-939-3

Dreams and Visions: Language of the Spirit

By Margaret M. Bowater

Dreams and Visions is an easy-to-follow, practical, and inspirational guide that provides a background to the nature and range of dreams and reveals the power of dream interpretation.

$14.95 • Paper • ISBN 0-89594-966-0

Fundamentals of Tibetan Buddhism

By Rebecca McClen Novick

This book explores the history, philosophy, and practice of Tibetan Buddhism. Novick's concise history of Buddhism, and her explanations of the Four Noble Truths, Wheel of Life, Karma, Five Paths, Six Perfections, and the different schools of thought within the Buddhist teachings help us understand Tibetan Buddhism as a way of experiencing the world, more than as a religion or philosophy.

$12.95 • Paper • ISBN 0-89594-953-9

BOOKS BY THE CROSSING PRESS

Pocket Guide to Meditation
By Alan Pritz

This book focuses on meditation as part of spiritual practice, as a universal tool to forge a deeper connection with spirit. In Alan Pritz's words, Meditation simply delivers one of the most purely profound experiences of life, joy.

$6.95 • Paper • ISBN 0-89594-886-9

Pocket Guide to The Tarot
By Alan Oken

The Tarot has been an ancient source of wisdom and insight into the human heart and mind. The 78 cards of the Tarot deck help you to open a door to higher consciousness, gain insights on the past and present, and discern future directions.

$6.95 • Paper • ISBN 0-89594-822-2

Soul-Centered Astrology: A Key to Your Expanding Self
By Alan Oken

Complete with detailed astrological charts and diagrams, meditations, and visualizations, this is the definitive guide to enlightenment for professional and amateur astrologers alike.

$18.95 • Paper • ISBN 0-89594-811-7

Secrets of a Jewish Baker
1994 James Beard award winner
By George Greenstein

... Greenstein's book is easily worth several times its price.—Vogue

$16.95 • Paper • ISBN 0-89594-605-X

To receive a current catalog from The Crossing Press
please call toll-free, 800-777-1048.
Visit our Web site: **www.crossingpress.com**